STUDIES IN ECONOMIC AND SOCIAL HISTORY

This series, specially commissioned by the Economic History Society, provides a guide to the current interpretations of the key themes of economic and social history in which advances have recently been made or in which there has been significant debate.

Originally entitled 'Studies in Economic History', in 1974 the series had its scope extended to include topics in social history, and the new series title, 'Studies in Economic and Social History', signalises this development.

The series gives readers access to the best work done, helps them to draw their own conclusions in major fields of study, and by means of the critical bibliography in each book guides them in the selection of further reading. The aim is to provide a springboard to further work rather than a set of pre-packaged conclusions or short-cuts.

ECONOMIC HISTORY SOCIETY

The Economic History Society, which numbers around 3000 members, publishes the *Economic History Review* four times a year (free to members) and holds an annual conference. Enquiries about membership should be addressed to the Assistant Secretary, Economic History Society, PO Box 190, 1 Greville Road, Cambridge CB1 3QG. Full-time students may join at special rates.

STUDIES IN ECONOMIC AND SOCIAL HISTORY

Edited for the Economic History Society by L.A. Clarkson

PUBLISHED

OTHER TITLES ARE IN PREPARATION

The Industrialisation of Russia, 1700–1914

Prepared for
The Economic History Society by

M. E. FALKUS

Lecturer in Economic History
in the London School of Economics
and Political Science

MACMILLAN

First published 1972
8th reprint 1989

Published by
MACMILLAN EDUCATION LTD
Houndmills, Basingstoke, Hampshire RG21 2XS
and London
Companies and representatives
throughout the world

Printed in Hong Kong

ISBN 0–333–11649–6

Contents

List of Tables

Editor's Preface

SO long as the study of economic history was confined to only a small group at a few universities, its literature was not prolific and its few specialists had no great problem in keeping abreast of the work of their colleagues. Even in the 1930s there were only two journals devoted exclusively to this field. But the high quality of the work of the economic historians during the inter-war period and the post-war growth in the study of the social sciences sparked off an immense expansion in the study of economic history after the Second World War. There was a great expansion of research and many new journals were launched, some specialising in branches of the subject like transport, business or agricultural history. Most significantly, economic history began to be studied as an aspect of history in its own right in schools. As a consequence, the examining boards began to offer papers in economic history at all levels, while textbooks specifically designed for the school market began to be published.

For those engaged in research and writing this period of rapid expansion of economic history studies has been an exciting, if rather breathless one. For the larger numbers, however, labouring in the outfield of the schools and colleges of further education, the excitement of the explosion of research has been tempered by frustration caused by its vast quantity and, frequently, its controversial character. Nor, it must be admitted, has the ability or willingness of the academic economic historians to generalise and summarise marched in step with their enthusiasm for research.

The greatest problems of interpretation and generalisation have tended to gather round a handful of principal themes in economic history. It is, indeed, a tribute to the sound sense of economic historians that they have continued to dedicate their energies, however inconclusively, to the solution of these key problems. The results of this activity, however, much of it stored away in a wide range of academic journals, have tended

9

to remain inaccessible to many of those currently interested in the subject. Recognising the need for guidance through the burgeoning and confusing literature that has grown around these basic topics, the Economic History Society decided to launch this series of small books. The books are intended to serve as guides to current interpretations in important fields of economic history in which important advances have recently been made, or in which there has recently been some significant debate. Each book aims to survey recent work, to indicate the full scope of the particular problem as it has been opened up by recent scholarship, and to draw such conclusions as seem warranted, given the present state of knowledge and understanding. The authors will often be at pains to point out where, in their view, because of a lack of information or inadequate research, they believe it is premature to attempt to draw firm conclusions. While authors will not hesitate to review recent and older work critically, the books are not intended to serve as vehicles for their own specialist views: the aim is to provide a balanced summary rather than an exposition of the author's own viewpoint. Each book will include a descriptive bibliography.

In this way the series aims to give all those interested in economic history at a serious level access to recent scholarship in some major fields. Above all, the aim is to help the reader to draw his own conclusions, and to guide him in the selection of further reading as a means to this end, rather than to present him with a set of pre-packaged conclusions.

M. W. FLINN
Editor

Bibliographical Note

REFERENCES in the text, footnotes and table sources within square brackets refer to the numbered items in the Bibliography, followed, where necessary, by the page number, e.g. ([49] 168).

1 Introduction

RUSSIA on the eve of the First World War could scarcely be regarded as an industrial country. Farming was still the occupation of the overwhelming majority of the population. Possibly two-thirds of those in employment were to be found in agriculture, and agriculture contributed almost one-half of the national income. Large towns existed, but they were few in number. In 1914 the urban population was only some 18 per cent of the total. Foreign trade, too, reflected the agrarian-based nature of the Russian economy. Finished manufactured products formed only some 5·6 per cent of total exports in 1913, while foodstuffs and agricultural semi-manufactured goods were in excess of 70 per cent. Imports of manufactures, by contrast, amounted to 22 per cent of the total. Agricultural productivity in this agricultural society was extremely low, and, in consequence, per capita incomes were small. Indeed, Russian national income per head was one of the lowest in Europe. The estimates in Table 1 (which are no more than rough guides) clearly demonstrate Russia's relative backwardness. In per capita terms, the United States was more than six times as wealthy as Russia in 1913, England about four and a half times, France three and a half, and Germany three times. Italy had a per capita income probably double that of Russia, while that of Austria-Hungary was also substantially higher. For figures comparable with Russia it is to nations like Romania and Bulgaria that we must turn.

Backwardness was reflected too in the low levels of education among the population. This factor, like so many other elements of backwardness, was both cause and effect of poor economic performance. In 1883 some four-fifths of the army recruits from certain southern districts could neither read nor write, while the average level of illiteracy in 1913 may still have been as high as 60 or 65 per cent of the total population.

There was much in the manufacturing sector of 1913, too,

11

TABLE 1

PER CAPITA NATIONAL INCOME OF SELECTED COUNTRIES, 1913
(gold roubles*)

United States	682·2	Italy	209·9
Australia	505·3	Austria-Hungary	174·9
Great Britain	446·6	Russia†	101·4
France	354·7	Bulgaria	97·2
Germany	300·1	Romania	97·2
Belgium	267·2		

SOURCE: [49] 168. Note that these estimates are not comparable with Western calculations, for they omit income generated by the service sector.

* The rouble was made convertible into gold in 1897 at a rate equal approximately to 2s. 1d. sterling. Before that date the rouble had fluctuated for long periods, but as a rough guide can be considered as equivalent to about 2s.

† Territory of pre-1939 U.S.S.R.

that seems more akin to a backward, primary-producing country, than to an advanced industrial one. Some 'modern' sectors, for example chemicals and machine-tools, had developed to only a very limited extent. Others, like electrical equipment and automobiles, were scarcely developed at all. Within 'large-scale' industry, mining was the chief branch of activity, both by employment and by the value of net product. Among manufacturers, food processing, textiles and metallurgy were the leading groups. Mining, food processing and cotton textiles taken together accounted for some 60 per cent of the value of net production of large-scale industrial enterprises. At the same time, a significant proportion of industrial output (probably at least one-third) was produced outside factory establishments, in the urban handicraft workshops and in peasant dwellings. These forms of industry (known as *remeslo* and *kustar* industry) lie largely outside the scope of official statistics, and much about their development remains obscure. Yet in 1900 they probably employed, though often on a part-time basis, at least 5 million workers, more than double the numbers in factory enterprises.

For all this, Russia possessed by 1913 a substantial industrial sector. In absolute size, Russia's industrial sector ranked fifth in

12

the world, after the United States, Germany, Britain and France. Russia's cotton-spinning industry, measured by the number of spindles, probably ranked fourth, after Britain, the United States and Germany. The linen industry occupied third place, behind Ireland and France. And Russia also had a well-developed heavy industrial sector. In coal and pig-iron Russian production was in fifth place, and in steel fourth (above France). Russian output of petroleum was second only to the United States, accounting for nearly 18 per cent of world production. On a per capita basis, of course, Russian production was much less impressive. Indeed, per capita industrial output in the United States was more than ten times that of Russia. Yet this illustrates an important point: for a country such as Russia, with a huge peasant population, per capita figures have only a limited value. Significant changes may well appear insignificant by virtue of the large denominator.

Tsarist industrial development has attracted a great deal of attention from historians, both Western and Soviet. Such studies are frequently influenced by wider considerations. For Marxist historians, industrial development has a central role in the general historical schema, for it is largely through industrial history that Marx analysed the unfolding of historical stages. For many non-Marxist scholars, too, industry is seen to play a critical part in the process of economic growth; thus studies of Russia frequently cast glances in the direction of this more general problem. Specifically, the Marxist may ask whether Russia in 1917 was 'ripe' for a socialist revolution, and he may seek for the necessary stages of 'industrial capitalism' and 'monopoly capitalism' in the preceding phases. The Western historian may ask whether Russian industrial growth after the Revolution was a product mainly of the new regime, or whether the Soviet Government was simply building on existing foundations. Was Russia, in fact, already launched on a path of industrialisation by 1914? The historian may seek for evidence of significant industrial development, possibly a 'take-off', in the earlier period. It is interesting that historians, both Marxist and non-Marxist, have concentrated on the development of large-scale industries, as shown in official statistics, despite the significance of small-scale manufacturing activity. Thus the term 'industrialisation' often has overtones of bigness of scale and modernity of organisation in manufacturing industry; it is not used to mean simply the development of a secondary sector.

The use of comparative history is often found in studies of Russian economic history. Gerschenkron has produced valuable insights into both Russian history and into general European history by his comparisons of Russian industrialisation with that found elsewhere.[1] Soviet historians likewise frequently make international comparisons, which generally either serve as elaborations of historical stages, or demonstrate Russia's extreme backwardness relative to other capitalist countries, in 1913. Another notable characteristic in Soviet studies of Tsarist economic history is an emphasis on economic crises and depressions. Thus, the problems of short-term capitalist growth – the trade cycle – rather than its long-run 'self-sustaining' nature have, not altogether surprisingly, attracted most attention.

Different standpoints produce different history, and one should bear this in mind when studying Russia. Soviet writers, for instance, are particularly concerned with the origins of economic phenomena. Lenin laid stress on the growth of the 'capitalist factory' during the feudal period, so an important place in the literature is reserved for discussing the origins of a free industrial labour force, the earliest development of large units of production, and the first uses of mechanical techniques. Such an emphasis is nowadays rather unfashionable among non-Marxist historians who, especially when concerned with the problem of long-term economic growth, tend to look for significant quantitative changes, for a 'take-off', an industrial 'spurt', and so on. There has thus been much research by Soviet scholars on industrial development prior to the Emancipation of the Serfs in 1861, whereas it is the subsequent period that has attracted most attention elsewhere. Again, Marxist historians are concerned with the institutional framework within which development took place, and this leads to debates which sometimes seem arid and even pointless to others. When did the capitalist 'manufactory' become a capitalist 'factory'? Were the state enterprises established by Peter the Great feudal or capitalist? Naturally

[1] See, for example, *Economic Backwardness in Historical Perspective* ([29] 5–30), and Lecture Three ([32] 62–96).

14

enough, historical periodisation is greatly influenced by considerations such as these. Soviet writers in general view the pre-Emancipation period as one in which the capitalist factory emerged out of feudalism. After the Emancipation came 'industrial capitalism', culminating, between 1900 and 1914, in the stage of 'monopoly capitalism'. Most Western writers would certainly agree that the year 1861 marked a turning-point in Russian economic history, but they would place less emphasis on the 'capitalist' development of the economy prior to this. The decade of the 1890s is generally regarded as a crucial period in Russian industrialisation because of the rapid rates of industrial growth then attained. Once again, the emphasis is on magnitudes rather than on institutional changes.

These, then, are some of the problems faced by a student of Russian economic history. There are others of a different nature. Tsarist statistics present a well-known hazard. The data come largely from official sources, collected by government departments. The collection of such material for industry began as far back as 1804, but the numerous defects – inexact and changing classifications and inaccurate data (government departments frequently relied until well into the nineteenth century on reports from provincial governors, who in turn obtained their information from local police and village priests) – make such statistics of dubious value. On occasions different government departments were able to produce quite contrary figures for apparently the same subject. And despite the voluminous data, spawned by the large Russian bureaucracy, numerous gaps exist. That most basic of sources, a population census, was taken only once during the whole Tsarist period, in 1897. Even this is known to have omitted entire provinces. In the same year also an industrial census was taken, providing information for 1887 and 1897, and further such data were collected in 1900, 1908 and 1912. Much useful information was provided by these censuses, although their coverage was far from complete. They left out, for example, most of the *remeslo* and *kustar* enterprises. For few industries is it possible to obtain adequate long-run output series. Only from 1890, for example, are there statistics of the physical production of cotton textiles; before this date, output has to be estimated from the consumption of cotton. However, the avail-

15

able statistics do yield much of value, as long as their weaknesses are borne in mind. Certainly their quality improved with time, and from the 1880s it is possible to use official data with much greater confidence.

Reflecting both the inadequacies of Tsarist statistics and the need for additional research, many fundamental economic indicators are known only vaguely, if at all. No annual series of national income estimates exist for the years before the Bolshevik Revolution, and no satisfactory estimate for any individual year before 1900. Thus the aggregate performance of the Russian economy over a long period cannot be assessed in any but the most tentative terms. Such topics as the behaviour of prices, the mobility of labour, the development of peasant and urban handicrafts, the growth of the internal market, the mobilisation of indigenous capital and entrepreneurship – these and many others require much further investigation.

A subject as vast as the industrialisation of Russia clearly cannot be treated adequately within the confines of a short pamphlet. Many important aspects are treated only sketchily or not at all, although the Bibliography will introduce interested students to reading of more depth and on wider subjects. Thus, there is no discussion of wages, prices, living standards, factory legislation or entrepreneurship. At the same time, knowledge of the general political and social background within which Russia industrialised, which is essential for an understanding of Russian industrialisation, has been largely taken for granted. But a few basic influences on Russian development may be briefly outlined. In the first place it is clear that Russia's population was growing rapidly from the beginning of the eighteenth century (see Table 2). This growth was partly due to natural increase but also to the extension of the Russian Empire into new territories. Greater population and the absorption of new regions stimulated growing commercial relations and specialisation. At various times Russia acquired relatively advanced regions and important new sources of raw materials. Thus in the second half of the eighteenth century the Polish provinces, the Ukraine and White Russia were obtained. During the reign of Peter the Great, Russia had acquired a maritime outlet on the Baltic, and during the 1770s the Black Sea was reached. Russia's huge land frontiers and the

TABLE 2

GROWTH OF POPULATION OF THE RUSSIAN EMPIRE,
1722–1913

Year	Total population (millions)
1722	14·0
1762	19·0
1800	35·5
1860	74·1
1897	126·4
1913	170·1

SOURCE: [13] 79, 434, 452–4.

conquest and defence of new territories necessitated a vast budget and a constant preoccupation with military affairs on the part of the Government. Politics went hand in hand with economics. During the eighteenth century, Russia emerged from the wings of Europe to take her place on the centre of the stage as a great power, and the role of government in the Russian economy and the impulse for state involvement in economic affairs provided by political pressures forms a continuing theme in Russian economic history. To a large extent several characteristic features of Russian economic backwardness – the persistence of serfdom, the huge military budget and the predominant influence of the state – can be traced to Russia's political expansion. The sparsely populated border regions were vulnerable to attack, while the possibility of peasant flights to remote regions encouraged the stricter imposition of servile status on the mass of the population both for fiscal and military reasons.

Russian industry thus developed within a poor agricultural society in which the overwhelming proportion of the population were serfs before 1861.[2] Internal demand for the products of Russian industry was consequently low, while serfdom also made the recruitment of an industrial labour force difficult. Subsistence agriculture and largely self-sufficient estates were characteristic of

[2] The term 'serf' is used here rather loosely to include not only those in personal bondage to the Russian gentry, but the almost equal numbers of state peasants. Thus defined, the serf population of Russia was about 60 per cent of the total in 1860.

large sections of the Russian economy in 1861. And the prosperity of the internal market that evolved continued to be strongly influenced by the state of the harvest and the course of agricultural prices down to the outbreak of the First World War.

It must not be thought that Tsarist Russia was a country well endowed with natural resources. The huge raw-materials base of Soviet industrial power does not indicate the resources available to the Tsars. Inadequate and expensive communications, sometimes with regions where hostile races made Russian control difficult, hampered the exploitation even of known resources. Not until the 1880s could the coal and iron of the Ukraine be worked on a large scale, and Siberia remained remote and largely uncolonised until the very end of the century. Indeed, the industrialisation of Russia before 1914 means for practical purposes the industrialisation of European Russia, and then of certain regions only. The huge variations in the economies, resources and levels of development that existed among different regions make generalisations about the performance of the Russian economy dangerous. If Russia's mineral resources were inadequate and often inaccessible before the advent of railways, her agriculture too was not well endowed by nature. Even the famed fertile black-soil belt of Great Russia and the steppes of the Ukraine and south-eastern Volga regions needed the development of communications before they could be fully exploited, while the vagaries of the climate meant frequent harvest failures.

Geographical and climatic factors, indeed, perpetuated backwardness in Russia. Vast distances between raw materials and markets meant high transport costs. Russia's Black Sea ports are far removed from the main population centres, while the Baltic ports freeze for several months every year. Russia possesses great river systems, such as the Volga, the Dnieper and the Don, but the majority of Russia's navigable rivers flow away from the main centres of economic activity. Thus the Volga flows to the Caspian Sea, the Dnieper and Don to the Black Sea. Moreover, in winter much of Russia's network of inland waterways froze, while during the spring thaw her rudimentary road system became a sea of mud. The long harsh winters, especially in northern regions, encouraged the widespread development of peasant handicrafts during the times when agricultural work became im-

18

possible. Such factors encouraged the continuance of local markets and small-scale rural manufacturing, and provided an obstacle to the introduction of modern industry in Russia.

A further general point to be emphasised is the international environment within which Russia industrialised. England, France and other Western European nations and regions were considerably more developed than Russia. Russia, although geographically and culturally remote from the West for a great deal of the period, could import Western technology and benefit from the contacts brought by trade and travel. Rostow's concept of a uniform 'traditional' society in nations before their industrial phase is not very helpful. Even at the opening of the eighteenth century, long before the industrial revolutions in the West, Russia was significantly more backward than these other countries, and throughout the entire period Russian industrialisation owed much to foreign technology, to foreign entrepreneurs and artisans, and, later, to foreign capital. And it was the striving on the part of the Russian state to emulate the economic strength of its competitors that led on occasions to significant advances in Russian industrialisation.

2   The Beginnings of Industrialisation

HOW far was Russia on the path to industrialisation at the time of Emancipation in 1861? The major developments, certainly, occurred after this time. It was only in the last two decades of the nineteenth century that a significant upturn in the pace of industrial growth becomes demonstrable, and it was in these years that much of Russia's industrial base – in particular the coal and iron of the south and the petroleum of the Caucasus – was laid. Yet a number of Soviet specialists have stressed the importance of changes which took place in the industrial sector prior to 1861. They have applied the term 'industrial revolution' to the period between the mid-1830s and the Emancipation, while Yakovlev has even argued for an industrial revolution in the period 1790–1825.[3] And Soviet historians in general are increasingly pointing to the eighteenth century as the origin of 'capitalist manufacture' in the country. Such an emphasis is a useful corrective to those accounts of Russian industrialisation which virtually ignore the earlier period, regarding the economy as 'traditional', and overlooking the significant developments which in fact took place. For during the years between the accession of Peter the Great (1682–1725) and the Emancipation, numerous changes had occurred in Russia's industrial structure, changes the more impressive in that they occurred within the institutional framework of a serf society.

In the economic sphere, as in so much else, the reign of Peter the Great marked a decisive break in Russian history. The last twenty-five years of Peter's life saw the growth of a substantial manufacturing sector which gave employment to several thousands of industrial workers. Old industries were expanded, and new ones introduced. Old centres of manufacturing were extended, new ones created. Foreign commerce grew and its main

[3] See, for example, Yakovlev [81]; the article by Yatsunsky in Rozhkova ([65] 118–220); also Yatsunsky [83], and Strumilin ([19] 390–413).

channel was shifted from the White Sea to the Baltic, from the ancient port of Archangel to Peter's newly-constructed capital at St Petersburg.

Certainly, industrial growth during the first quarter of the eighteenth century was not without earlier foundations. Some large-scale undertakings had made their appearance in the previous century. Ironworks had been established, initially by foreigners, from the 1630s. Here and there 'manorial (*votchinal*) factories', set up by estate owners and using the labour of their own serfs, existed. Self-sufficiency remained characteristic of the Russian village, but some regional specialisation was developing, and small-scale village handicrafts and peasant cottage industries were sometimes producing for a wide market. Such specialisation was found, for instance, in the iron products from the Tula and Moscow regions, in linens from Tver and Moscow, leather from Nizhni-Novgorod, and salt from the Kama and Upper Volga regions.

The industrial structure that emerged during the first quarter of the eighteenth century was fashioned almost entirely to state requirements. Peter's frequent wars provided the principal driving force and, especially in the early years, the state itself set up and operated numerous enterprises geared to military needs. Cannon foundries and armaments works were constructed, iron and copper mining developed, and geological surveys were initiated to discover mineral resources. Woollen-cloth factories were set up to provide uniforms for the armies, while sailcloth, rope and other manufactures were developed to provide equipment for the newly-formed navy.

The majority of these state enterprises were later sold or leased to private entrepreneurs, particularly after 1720, and the role of private enterprise in setting up new establishments increased as Peter's reign drew to a close. But the state played a dominant part even in the development of private works. Subsidies, tax exemptions, monopolies and other concessions were employed to encourage Russians to found manufacturing enterprises. And the state was far and away the main customer for the products of the new factories.

From the second decade of the century Peter's industrial policies were increasingly influenced by 'mercantilism'. With the object of lessening Russia's dependence on imported manufactures, Peter fostered a variety of industries such as glass, velvets, brocades and silk, some of these products being manufactured in Russia for the first time. In addition to the usual subsidies, a strongly protectionist policy was adopted under the 1724 tariff, under which a wide range of goods were subjected to duties ranging from 50 to 75 per cent *ad valorem.*

Industrial development under Peter thus bears the character of a 'forced industrialisation'. The achievements were impressive, although there is controversy over the actual quantitative results of Peter's industrialisation. At the beginning of the reign there probably existed some 21 'manufactories', of which 4 were run by the state. One estimate puts the number of new plants founded in Peter's reign as 233, but more recent research indicates lower figures. Zaozorskaya puts the total at 178, of which 40 were for armaments and iron metallurgy and 15 for non-ferrous metallurgy; there were also 23 sawmills, 15 woollen-cloth factories and 13 tanneries.[4] Of these enterprises, nearly half were established by the state. The composition of Peter's industries reflected both the state's needs and the extreme backwardness of the country. Nearly all the new enterprises were founded to meet the state's demands, a few to serve the luxury demands of the nobility (a market itself influenced by Peter's Westernising policies). A mass market did not exist, for as long as the country was tied to a regime of serfdom and as long as agricultural productivity remained low a prosperous domestic demand could not grow.

Here, then, are some of the threads for an interpretation of Russian industrial history put forward by Gerschenkron.[5] In a very backward country substantial industrialisation cannot take place on the basis of mass demand, private domestic capital and available entrepreneurial resources. The state, if it desires industrialisation, has to foster industries. At the same time, according to Gerschenkron, it was a characteristic of Russia that state measures to promote industry produced a further retarding

[4] These statistics are quoted by Polyanskii ([15] 139–40); see also Gerschenkron ([32] 72).

[5] See, for example, 'Russia: Patterns and Problems of Economic Development, 1861–1958' ([29] 119–51).

22

force, a new dimension of backwardness. In Peter the Great's time came the strengthening of serfdom, the crushing taxation on the peasants (a poll tax was introduced in 1716), and various other adverse factors which increased the already powerful forces in the economy resistant to spontaneous industrial growth. In the latter part of the nineteenth century, as we shall see, industrialisation was again pursued at the cost of internal purchasing power, and at the cost, in consequence, of the spontaneous development of internal demand.

Among the positive results of Peter's 'forced industrialisation' were the foundation of important new centres of mining and metallurgy in the mountain regions of the Urals, the strengthening of various industries in the Moscow region, particularly textiles, and the creation of a wholly new centre of manufacturing in St Petersburg. By the end of Peter's reign a substantial proportion of cloth for army uniforms was produced by Russian factories, and dependence on imports over a wide range of manufactures had been lessened. St Petersburg possessed not only factories supplying the needs of the army and navy but also those catering for the demands of Peter's court. In 1700 Russia had been an importer of iron; by 1716 she was a net exporter, and later in the century became the world's largest iron producer. In the Urals some 76 ironworks were in operation by 1725, and by the end of Peter's reign the annual production of the Urals works amounted to some 800,000 poods[6] of pig-iron. By this time state enterprises were joined by private concerns, some of them, such as those belonging to the Demidov family, operating on a very large scale.

Nearly all the private entrepreneurs came from members of the merchant class, and a number of Marxist historians, such as Tugan-Baranovsky and Lyashchenko, have taken this as evidence that Russia by the opening of the eighteenth century had reached the stage of 'commercial capitalism'. One must not exaggerate, however, either the availability of capital or the amounts required by Peter's industries. Some historians have drawn attention to the chronic shortage of capital in Russia at the time, and have pointed out that the state played a major

[6] 1 pood = approx. 36 lb. (16·3 kg.).

part in subsidising even the private establishments. Moreover, the enterprises themselves were often exceedingly small, employing only a handful of workers and little fixed capital. Certain enterprises, it is true, were very large. Thus a sailcloth factory in Moscow employed 1,162 workers, and a state woollen-cloth factory in Miklayev employed 742, while a private cloth factory in Shchegolin had a labour force of 730. The largest works were evidently to be found in the Urals iron industries, and the mining enterprises in the province of Perm employed some 25,000. But some of the big enterprises were in reality more like colonies of domestic handicraft workers, working for a single employer, than large-scale factories. Kulisher, in contrast to writers such as Tugan-Baranovsky and Liubimirov, has emphasised the small-scale character of Peter's enterprises.

In any event, the development of industries in the first quarter of the eighteenth century imposed severe problems for the backward Russian economy. The acute shortage of skilled labour was solved, to some extent, by the introduction of foreigners. Peter here, as in so many of his industrial policies, continued the policies of his predecessors but on a considerably enhanced scale. Returning from his first European visit in 1698, Peter brought back hundreds of foreign technicians and skilled artisans, and encouraged foreign entrepreneurs to set up establishments in Russia. Young Russians were sent to Europe to learn the secrets of Western industrial processes.

A further major problem was the recruiting of labour for the new enterprises. The grip of serfdom had increased in Russia during the seventeenth century, and there was no group in the stratified society that had emerged which could form the basis of an industrial labour force. Some free labour did exist, but on an inadequate scale for the new industries. Peter tackled the problem in part by drafting criminals and beggars to the factories. At the same time, state peasants were ascribed in large numbers to enterprises, both state and private. And – a new departure – merchants were allowed to purchase serfs for industrial labour. The latter concession was generalised in a law of 1721 which permitted merchants to buy whole villages for their enterprises. Such serfs did not become the property of the purchaser, however, but became the property of the industrial enter-

24

prise and would remain with the enterprise if ownership changed hands. These people became known as 'possessional peasants', and their conditions and treatment were frequently far worse than those of agricultural serfs. Possessional factories were particularly important in the Urals industries, where the problems of recruiting a labour force were most acute.

Peter thus solved the problems of industrial labour by extending serfdom to industry. The growth of industry went hand in hand with the further depression of the status of Russian peasants and with further rigidities in the social composition of Russian society. The influence of the state in industrialisation had consequences which were felt until the time of the Emancipation and beyond. Market forces could operate to only a limited extent in obtaining a supply of industrial labour. In numerous private manufacturing establishments the various government concessions and privileges, as well as the regulations that accompanied the establishment of possessional factories, involved the state bureaucracy in detailed administration and control. The financing of Peter's industrial and military activities led to greater and greater burdens on the servile population, and the poll tax was to remain in force for more than thirty years after the Emancipation.

3 Economic Development after Peter the Great

PETER the Great's industrialisation policies have been discussed in some detail because they bring out important general factors in Russian economic history. It should be obvious that Russian society was very different from that in the West, and its problems were correspondingly distinct. Russia was more backward than her Western neighbours, and only the state could mobilise the capital and entrepreneurship and provide a market sufficient for a major increase in the tempo of industrial development. Russia's political aspirations necessitated the establishment of certain industries; the realities of Russian backwardness dictated an institutional framework (such as the possessional factory and the strengthening of serfdom) which imposed further rigidities on the economy.

Debate has arisen over the fate of Peter's industries in the years following his death.[7] Older Marxist historians like Pokrovsky and Kliuchevsky have argued that after 1725 most of Peter's industries collapsed, and that the Russian economy entered a period of stagnation at least until the accession of Catherine II (1762–96). The main evidence for such a decline was the failure of numerous enterprises, for by 1760 only a small number of the original two hundred or so establishments were still in existence.

Recently, however, the view of sharp decline has undergone revision. Continuity of economic activity after Peter has been stressed by Kahan and by a number of Soviet historians. Kahan has argued that the figures of industrial failures are misleading, for they occurred mainly among the smaller enterprises. Moreover, continuance of operation was sometimes masked by changes of ownership. In any case, some failures would be expected in the normal course of business operations, especially as the onset of peace after 1725 inevitably involved difficulties for the many firms engaged directly or indirectly in the manufacture of military equipment.

[7] See the discussion of this problem and the bibliographical references in Kahan [46].

Some branches of industry continued to make substantial progress after 1725, particularly the mining and metallurgical industries of the Urals. According to Strumilin the output of pig-iron grew steadily after the first quarter of the eighteenth century, with the output of private plants outstripping that of state-owned works. Especially in the reign of Elizabeth (1741–61), large numbers of Urals works were transferred from state to private ownership, usually on extremely favourable terms to the purchasers. By the middle of the eighteenth century, when the Urals accounted for some 65 per cent of Russian iron output and 90 per cent of her copper, Russia was by far the world's major iron producer (see Table 3). A large export trade to England was developed, and the trade continued to grow in the second half of the century.

TABLE 3

GROWTH OF PIG-IRON PRODUCTION IN RUSSIA, 1700–1800
('000 poods)

Year	Output	Year	Output
1700	150	1760	3,663
1710	316	1770	5,106
1720	610	1780	6,718
1730	957	1790	7,957
1740	1,530	1800	9,908
1750	2,009		

SOURCE: [23] 180, 197, 204.

Light industries too made progress after Peter's death, especially in the Moscow region and in the province of Vladimir. Substantial centres of small-scale manufacture of linens, leather products, basketwares, wood products, food processing and many other products developed.

It is probably best to view the period between the death of Peter and the accession of Catherine II as one of steady, though not spectacular, industrial growth. During Catherine's reign, rather more rapid growth seems to have set in. Alongside the growth of relatively large industrial enterprises, the expansion of which is the indicator of industrialisation used by Soviet historians, went an increase of artisan and *kustar* manu-

27

facturing. In general, the larger industries catered for the needs of the state, the nobility, clergy and government officials. Small-scale and household manufacture met the needs of the mass of the population. Certainly, by 1800 the sway of the self-sufficient estate had lessened significantly, although it had far from disappeared. Regional specialisation evolved on a considerable scale. For example, the village of Pavlov in Nizhni-Novgorod province had 323 metal-fabricating workshops by 1800. Numerous textile enterprises existed in Ivanovo, Moscow, Saratov and other centres.

Among the factors underlying the growth of industries, population increase was of fundamental importance. Russia's population more that doubled between the 1740s and the 1790s, and population increase and the acquisition of new territories fostered internal trade and a territorial division of labour. By the end of the century a quite clear demarcation had arisen between the industrial areas in the north and around Moscow, and the agricultural regions to the south. Towns grew, although the urban population still constituted only a tiny fraction of the total. In 1724 the urban population accounted for only 3 per cent of the total, according to one estimate. At the end of the century it still accounted for little more than 4 per cent.

Government policies continued to favour industrial development. Internal commercial restrictions were gradually relaxed, and in 1753 internal customs duties were abolished. Protection continued at a high level for much of the eighteenth century, although there were tariff reductions during Catherine's reign. Monopolies and privileges were bestowed on industrialists by Peter's immediate successors. Under the Empresses Anna (1730–40) and Elizabeth, the favoured industrialists were more often members of the nobility and court favourites rather than the prosperous merchants of Peter's time. Indeed, there was probably a relative decline in the role of merchants in Russian industrialisation as the century progressed. Certainly, labour recruitment proved an enduring problem for them, especially when restrictions were placed on the purchase of possessional peasants. In 1762 merchants were prohibited from buying serfs, although exceptions seem to have been made subsequently. The second half of the eighteenth century was the golden age of the

28

manorial factory operated by serf labour. Especially where landowners had ready access to raw materials, as in the manufacture of wool, linen and paper, they came to control a large share of total output. In the case of silk, leather and cotton, however, merchant manufacture predominated. Recent Soviet writers tend to emphasise the importance of 'capitalist' manufacture in Catherine's reign, especially in consumer-goods industries.[8] Such enterprises came increasingly to use hired, as opposed to compulsory, serf labour. This 'voluntary' labour was in fact provided by serfs who paid their owners' dues in money or kind (*obrok*) rather than by performing labour services (*barshchina*); thus, out of their industrial earnings, they could pay their obligations.

There also existed by the end of the eighteenth century certain industrial enterprises controlled by serfs. These were found in *obrok* areas, and employees in such enterprises came in the main from among *obrok* peasants. The most celebrated cases of serf entrepreneurship were found among Count Sheremetov's peasants in the village of Ivanovo in the province of Vladimir, where a handful of linen-weaving works in the mid-eighteenth century proved the foundation of a large and important textile centre in the course of the following century.

It is possible to compile an impressive list of the achievements of Russian industry during the course of the eighteenth century. According to Strumilin, the numbers of industrial enterprises had risen from about 200 at the end of Peter's reign to over 650 by the 1760s. Employment in these enterprises was estimated at 81,780 and the total value of production at 8·7 million roubles. At the opening of the nineteenth century there were recorded rather more than 2,000 enterprises producing goods valued at 18·0 million roubles, while the mining sector accounted for a further 200 enterprises. In all, the industrial labour force had risen to about 200,000, of which almost exactly half worked for wages. Most spectacular was the development of iron production. Output in the middle of the eighteenth century was about 2 million poods of pig-iron; by 1800 it reached 9·9 million poods.

[8] See, for example, the chapter by Polyanskii on Russian economic development, 1725–1800 ([15] 145–73).

It must be emphasised, however, that such developments hardly alter the picture of Russia as a backward, agrarian country. Many of the enterprises counted in the statistics as 'industrial establishments' were minute, employing only a handful of workers. Indeed, of the estimated 2,300 such establishments at the beginning of the nineteenth century, only about one-half employed more than sixteen workers. Even the existence of very large enterprises indicates more a response to the problems of organising a serf work-force, especially in remote areas like the Urals where control was difficult and the flight of workers always in prospect, than it does a response to the growth of capitalist enterprise. Certainly, 'large-scale' did not mean capital-intensity. Technology remained on an exceedingly low level. In the Urals, charcoal furnaces and handicraft methods of production held sway. Some Soviet historians, it is true, argue that Russia was not backward in the mid-eighteenth century by comparison with other European countries. They emphasise, for example, Russia's lead in iron production. But such a position is hardly tenable if one takes into account the low levels of productivity that existed throughout Russian industry.

Russian industry at the end of the eighteenth century thus presents a somewhat bewildering patchwork. There were state enterprises, using the ascribed labour of state peasants; *votchinal* enterprises, using serf labour; merchant enterprises, using both hired labour and possessional peasants, the latter especially significant in the Urals; serf enterprises, using hired labour; and, of course, the myriad small rural and village handicraft manufactures. The development of industries certainly indicates that despite serfdom the economy was by no means stagnant and inflexible. On one level were the state-run and state-aided enterprises, but on another was the spontaneous development of a few 'capitalist' industries, producing mainly consumer goods. The problem of labour supply was not so intractable as might be expected because of the possibility of hiring *obrok* peasants. And, despite the prevailing poverty and consequent low level of internal demand, there was undoubtedly a growth of regional specialisation and of internal commerce based on the domestic market for consumer goods.

4 Industrial Development, 1800–1861

AS for the eighteenth century, so for the first half of the nineteenth, there has been a reaction against the former emphasis on Russia's backwardness and stagnation. There is general agreement that the first quarter of the century saw only a low level of economic activity and that industrial progress was sluggish. These were years of considerable economic difficulties, with the Napoleonic Wars and their aftermath inevitably disrupting Russia's economy. Moreover, the period between 1816 and 1821 was one of low tariffs in Russia, and Russia's industries faced severe competition in these years from the growing industrial nations of Western Europe.

But the view that Russian industry was in a state of stagnation until the Emancipation of the Serfs has undergone considerable modification as a result of research by Soviet scholars. The Western historian Florinsky, in his well-known textbook [10], adheres to the traditional approach, stressing the limited nature of Russian development before 1860.[9] Strumilin, Yatsunsky, Rozhkova and others, on the other hand, write of an 'industrial revolution' taking place in Russia in the thirty years or so prior to the Emancipation. The evidence supporting an industrial revolution rests largely on the rapid progress of certain industrial sectors, the development of completely new industries, the beginnings of mechanisation in factories, and the marked acceleration in the use of 'free' labour by capitalist enterprises. The possessional and *votchinal* establishments showed an absolute decline during the second quarter of the century, especially from the 1840s.

It is not difficult to demonstrate a general quickening in the pace of economic activity, particularly from the 1830s. The

[9] Florinsky also denies significant economic progress in the eighteenth century after 1725. He writes: '. . . the state of economic stagnation that set in under Peter I's immediate successors continued throughout the later part of the century' ([11] 228).

buoyancy of internal trade is shown by the increasing turnover at the numerous fairs, which provided the main arteries for domestic commerce in the period. The most important fair was held annually at Nizhni-Novgorod, where merchants from all over Russia gathered. In 1863 the turnover at this fair accounted for about one-quarter of the total of more than 6,000 fairs, so that the prosperity of Nizhni-Novgorod provides a reasonably satisfactory indicator of the development of internal trade in Russia. In 1829 goods to the value of 28·2 million silver roubles were brought to the Nizhni-Novgorod fair; in 1834 their value was 39·2 million, and reached 103·3 million in 1859. Foreign trade, too, showed a sharp increase. Exports rose from about 63 million silver roubles in 1820 to 181 million at the time of the Emancipation, while over the corresponding period imports rose from 70 million silver roubles to 159 million. Strumilin emphasises the growth in membership of the urban merchant guilds as an indicator of increased economic activity. During the period of liberal tariffs after 1816 their numbers declined significantly, and there was a further falling-off in the late 1820s. However, between 1830 and 1855 the number of merchants belonging to guilds more than doubled, the 1850s witnessing a particularly sharp expansion. The period saw also improvements in communications. A number of important canals were constructed in the Baltic provinces at the opening of the nineteenth century, and by the 1850s steam navigation was developing rapidly on Russia's inland waterways, above all on the Volga. And in the 1830s came the beginnings of railway construction.

Associated with the growth of internal trade was a growing demarcation between the food-deficient areas of the industrial centre and the Baltic regions in the north, and the food-surplus regions of the black-earth and southern provinces. The self-sufficient estates with their manorial 'factories' declined in importance. It was in the less fertile northern regions where handicraft industries flourished that the *obrok* system of serf payments prevailed. By contrast, labour services predominated on the gentry estates in the grain-producing areas, especially in the black-earth provinces and in the Ukranian steppes. Thus, in European Russia the proportion of serfs performing labour services averaged rather more than 70 per cent in the first half of the nineteenth century. In the non-black-earth belt of central Russia, however, nearly 60 per cent of the serfs were on *obrok*. The general progress of industry can be seen from official statistics of the numbers of manufacturing plants and the growth of the labour force (see Table 4). From the 2,400 or so such

TABLE 4

ENTERPRISES AND LABOUR FORCE IN SELECTED INDUSTRIES,
1804–60

	Number of enterprises			Number of workers		
Commodity	1804	1830	1860	1804	1830	1860
1. Woollen textiles	157	389	706	28,689	67,241	120,025
2. Cotton textiles	199	538	1,200	8,181	76,228	152,236
3. Linen textiles	285	190	117	23,711	26,845	17,284
4. Silk manufacture	365	234	393	9,161	14,019	14,287
5. Paper	64	111	207	5,957	10,260	12,804
6. Leather	843	1,619	2,515	6,304	10,547	14,151
7. Tallow, soap, candles, wax	269	1,031	1,827	687	6,252	12,122
8. Sugar	10	57	467	108	1,687	64,763
9. Iron and steel	28	198	693	4,121	19,889	54,832
10. Copper	37	113	161	546	3,103	8,504

SOURCE: [13] 31–2.

establishments in 1804, the number had grown to 5,306 in 1830, and reached 15,338 in 1860. Correspondingly, the work-force grew from about 95,000 to 252,253, and finally to 565,100. Textiles remained the predominant sector in manufacturing industry, although the overall percentage of workers employed in textiles declined somewhat as metal-processing and other industries grew in importance. There appears, too, to have been a considerable increase in industrial productivity per worker, particularly after 1845, and this, according to Khromov, is associated with the growth of a voluntary labour force in manufacturing as well as the adoption of mechanisation. The late 1850s also produced a sharp increase in the numbers of joint-stock companies. Between 1822 and 1855, 32 such corporations had been established; from 1856 to 1859 a further 79 were formed. Some indication of the growth of mechanisation can be gleaned from the statistics shown in Table 5, although these figures include agricultural as well as industrial machinery.

TABLE 5

MACHINERY IN RUSSIA, 1831–60
('000 silver roubles)

Years	Machinery imports	Domestic production	Total
1831–40	4,111	2,750	6,861
1841–50	11,747	4,860	16,607
1851–60	48,080	36,433	84,513

SOURCE: [16] 27.

The growth of industries and the widening of the commercial nexus was reflected in increased urbanisation. According to Rashin, the urban population more than doubled in the period 1811–63 and the proportion of town dwellers in the total population of European Russia (excluding Poland and Finland) rose from 6·6 to 10 per cent (see Table 6). Moscow, St Petersburg

TABLE 6

URBAN POPULATION, 50 PROVINCES OF EUROPEAN RUSSIA, 1811–1913

Year	Population (millions)	Urban population (millions)	% Urban
1811	41·8	2·8	6·6
1838	48·8	4·5	9·3
1863	61·2	6·1	10·0
1885	81·7	10·0	12·2
1897	93·4	12·1	12·9
1913	121·8	18·6	15·3

SOURCE: [58] 98.

and Kiev grew rapidly, although the most spectacular expansion was that of Odessa, based on the development of the Black Sea grain trade (see Table 7).

Most of Russia's industrial production outside Poland was concentrated in four regions. The Urals continued as the main centre

34

TABLE 7

GROWTH OF CERTAIN TOWNS, 1811–1914
('000)

	1811	1863	1897	1914*
St Petersburg	335·6	539·5	1,264·9	2,118·5
Moscow	270·2	462·5	1,038·6	1,762·7
Riga	32·0	77·5	282·2	558·0
Kiev	23·3	68·4	247·7	520·5
Odessa	11·0	119·0	403·8	499·5
Baku	–	13·9	111·9	232·2
Ekaterinoslav	8·6	19·9	112·8	211·1

SOURCE: [58] 93.

*Population on 1 January 1914.

of mining and metallurgy. In the so-called 'Central Industrial Region' the provinces of Moscow and Vladimir contained important centres of textile manufacture. To the north, in the St Petersburg district, were found some of the largest metal-processing and cotton-textile plants. These northern industries benefited from the accessibility of imported goods such as coal, cotton and machinery, and St Petersburg also contained several large state manufacturing enterprises, including the famous Alexandrovsk works which produced Russia's earliest steam engines and railway equipment. According to Tegoborskii's estimate for the mid-1850s, rather more than half of the total value of the output of Russian manufacturing enterprises was concentrated in the provinces of Moscow, St Petersburg, Vladimir and Perm. In the south also several industrial regions of some importance developed, based principally on the refining of sugar from sugar-beet. Beyond Russia proper were a number of manufacturing centres in the Polish provinces. Lodz became a major textile producer, while Warsaw developed important metal-processing industries in addition to textiles.

Despite the shortcomings of Tsarist statistics, there can be no doubt that manufacturing industry grew substantially in the decades prior to 1861, although the significance and extent of these achievements can be debated. The causes of the increase are not fully understood, for despite the large volume of Soviet literature on the subject, little analysis of the dynamics of the expansion has been attempted. Certainly, however, industrial development in the first half of the nineteenth century was not a product of state initiative or pressure, and the period thus provides a strong contrast both with eighteenth-century industrialisation and with the achievements under Sergei Witte at the close of the nineteenth century. Many of the leading officials who served Nicholas I (1825–55) were either lukewarm in their support of industrial growth, or were actively hostile to it, fearing the social disturbances which might be involved. Count Kankrin, the powerful Minister of Finance who dominated economic policies between the mid-1820s and the early 1840s, was conservative by nature and interested primarily in fiscal matters. He viewed with suspicion proposals for state-sponsored industrial projects, while the Director of Transport, Tol', opposed the introduction of railways in the 1830s.

In view of the passive role of the state, it is not surprising that industrial advance during the decades before the Emancipation was most marked in consumer-goods industries, a feature which again contrasts with industrialisation under Peter the Great and Witte. Three general factors underlying the growth of industries in this period may be singled out. There was, in the first place, the expansion and increasing commercialisation of agriculture. The period saw a rapid extension of cultivation in the south-eastern provinces of New Russia, and exports of grain, especially wheat, rose sharply. Thus in 1820 the value of wheat exports amounted to some 7 million silver roubles; in 1840 they stood at 11 million, and in 1860 at over 37 million. The volume of all grain exports nearly doubled between the decades 1835–45 and 1845–55, while from about 15 per cent of the total value of exports prior to 1846, grain averaged roughly one-third between 1846 and 1860. Such growth could not fail to be reflected in internal demand for industrial products, while the development of the south and south-east as Russia's 'granary' stimulated territorial specialisation, as we have seen. Furthermore, the encouragement that this division of labour gave to the growth of *obrok* rather than labour services among serfs in the central and northern areas produced a potential labour force for Russia's manufacturing industries.

36

A second factor encouraging industrial development during the period was tariff protection. Import substitution, following the imposition of high tariffs in 1822, was a feature of many of those industrial sectors which grew most rapidly in Russia. Protection of infant industries was not, however, deliberate government policy. The main object of high tariffs was to increase state revenues, and the industrial expansion they sparked off was largely a by-product of fiscal policy.

The third factor was the spread of industrialisation in Western Europe. Russian industries could benefit from the improved techniques and machinery developed abroad, while the expanding demand for foodstuffs and raw materials from the industrialising nations provided opportunities for Russian exporters. A marked increase in Russia's grain exports to England followed in the wake of the repeal of the Corn Laws there in 1846. In these years before 1861 Russia entered increasingly into the growing international economy, as Strumilin has clearly shown in his study of the influence of the international trade cycle on Russian prosperity from the 1830s.[10]

Foremost among Russia's expanding industries was cotton textiles. During the 1830s cotton textiles overtook woollens as the major employer of industrial labour, and the widespread, peasant-based linen industry went into decline in the face of competition from cotton goods. Of the increase in Russia's industrial labour force between 1825 and 1834, nearly half was accounted for by cotton textiles.

Calico printing and weaving had made some headway in the eighteenth century, but in 1820 the scale of operations was still modest. Spinning had made little progress, and until the 1830s yarn imports were always larger than imports of raw cotton. Up to this time Russia's cotton industry was essentially the weaving and finishing of yarn imported from England, the processing being carried on primarily in peasant homes and in small handicraft workshops. From the 1830s the rate of growth of cotton textiles quickened, and the proportion of all 'factory' workers employed by this industry had risen to 32 per cent by

[10] Strumilin's study, covering the period 1847–1907, is reprinted in [19] 414–58; there is an English translation of the first section (up to 1867) in [68].

1836. From the 1840s cotton spinning developed rapidly, with much of the yarn produced in mechanised factories. One estimate of the increase in spindles employed in cotton spinning shows a rise from under 100,000 in 1830 to 1,750,000 in 1863, and by the time of the Emancipation over 90 per cent of Russia's yarn consumption was produced domestically (see Table 8). Mechanisation made much slower progress in weaving and it was not until the 1860s and 1870s that power-looms were widely adopted.

TABLE 8

IMPORTS OF COTTON, 1812–60
('000 poods)

Years	Cotton yarn	Raw cotton
1812–20	165	55
1821–30	334	87
1831–40	574	235
1841–50	471	821
1851–60	167	2,145

SOURCE: [1] I 527.

The main centres of spinning were in Moscow and St Petersburg. St Petersburg possessed the largest mills, and by 1860 many of them were organised as joint-stock companies. The major bleaching and printing factories were situated in the Moscow region and in the towns of Ivanovo and Shuya in the province of Vladimir. The rise of Ivanovo as an industrial centre has been traced by Yatsunsky [84]. Here a number of entrepreneurs, most of them serfs, set up linen-cloth enterprises from the 1740s. By the end of the century some of these enterprises had been turned over to the printing of cottons. Calico production then made rapid strides in the town, and by 1828 there existed over a hundred separate establishments, most of them, it is true, operating on a very small scale. Concentration of production increased, however, and by 1849, when one entrepreneur alone employed 2,459 workers, the twenty-two largest concerns employed five-sixths of all the calico workers in Ivanovo.

The main stimuli to Russia's cotton industry came from tariff protection, lower costs of yarn imports from England, and, after 1842, the greater availability of imported machinery from England. High tariffs in 1822 and 1826 gave a marked boost to the industry, and further impetus came in 1830 when a heavy duty was erected against Polish goods in the aftermath of the Polish uprising of that year. Tariffs remained high throughout the 1830s and 1840s, but starting in 1850 they were moderated, and a substantial downward revision followed in 1857. By this time, however, the industry was firmly established. Probably of even more significance than protective tariffs was the encouragement given to the weaving industry by the availability of cheap yarn imports from England. As the mechanisation of England's industries resulted in lower costs, the average price per pood of English yarn imported into Russia fell from 111 roubles in 1821–5 to an average of 82 roubles in the years 1826–30, and to 59 roubles in 1830–5. Cotton spinning was, of course, hindered by this price reduction, and although some progress was made during the 1830s, the main expansion came after 1842 when England lifted its ban on the exports of textile machinery. Encouragement was also supplied by an increased rate of duty on imported yarn in 1841, and over the next few decades cotton spinning developed rapidly on the basis of English technology and equipment. An important part in this process was played by a German-English entrepreneur, Ludwig Knoop, who set up and equipped the majority of the large cotton-textile mills in Russia in this period.

A notable feature of the cotton-textile industry was that from the outset it was based almost entirely on 'free' labour, that is, chiefly on the labour of *obrok* serfs. As early as 1825 some 95 per cent of the labour force was recruited in this manner, compared with an average for Russian industry as a whole of 54 per cent. Soviet historians lay considerable stress on this expansion of hired labour, using it as evidence of the growth of capitalist forms of enterprise within the 'feudal' structure of pre-Reform Russia. By 1860, 87 per cent of Russia's industrial workers were wage-earners. But it should be remembered that 'free' labour was free in only a restricted sense; personal bondage and obligations of the serf to his master continued, and the serf could always be recalled from his industrial employment.

A second new industry of importance to develop in the half-century before 1860 was sugar-beet production. As with cotton textiles, expansion here was in part the unwitting result of the 1822 tariff, and output became increasingly concentrated in substantial enterprises in the Ukraine during the 1840s and 1850s. The first sugar-beet refineries were established in the central provinces after 1802, but not until 1827 did the industry spread to the Ukraine. Initially these enterprises operated on a small scale, mostly as manorial factories using serf labour. After 1840 the adoption of steam-powered machinery led to larger units of production, and on the eve of the Emancipation mechanised factories accounted for 85 per cent of total output. The growth of production was impressive. Between 1844 and 1860 output grew from about 484,000 poods to 1,300,000 poods of sugar, while the Ukrainian region possessed 229 refineries by 1852, more than half the total in Russia at that date. Kiev, largely on the basis of sugar-beet, developed as a substantial manufacturing centre, and the industrial labour force there grew from some 1,500 in 1815 to over 32,000 in 1860.

Alongside the new industries, many of the older sectors of Russian industry made significant progress. Woollens, silk manufactures, paper production, and a host of small-scale craft industries connected with the processing of hides, wood and metals, all grew, although the linen industry declined, as mentioned earlier. In general, however, Russia's consumer-goods industries flourished, especially from the middle of the 1840s. Such was not the case with the iron industry, the great growth sector of the eighteenth century, which stagnated throughout the first half of the nineteenth century. Pig-iron production stood at some 12·2 million poods in 1806, whereas the average for the decades 1831–40 and 1841–50 was only 10·7 and 11·7 million poods respectively. Thereafter came a period of rapid growth, with production in 1860 totalling about 18·2 million poods. Yet over the entire period iron production failed to keep pace with the growth of population.

The iron industry remained centred in the Urals during this period, the enterprises there accounting for some three-quarters of total production. The prolonged stagnation in the Urals industries was a product of many factors. At the close of the eighteenth century the rapid expansion in England's domestic iron production had closed an important export outlet to Russian producers. Moreover, the system of forced labour which characterised the Urals plants led to low productivity, and labour unrest was a recurring feature from the second half of the eighteenth century. The contrast between the 'free' labour of cotton textiles and the serf labour of iron production, where possessional enterprises predominated until the Emancipation, was striking. Lyashchenko considers inefficient labour to be the principal cause of stagnation in the iron industry during the first half of the nineteenth century, yet the sparseness of population in the mountainous mining districts would have made the acquisition of a labour force other than by compulsion difficult and costly. Certainly, the archaic possessional enterprises with their unwilling labour and rigid bureaucratic control of all aspects of their operations were inefficient and unproductive. Coke smelting and the use of steam power were virtually unknown before the Emancipation; puddling was not introduced until the 1830s, and even in 1860 only one-half of the iron output was puddled.

The remoteness of the Urals from the main centres of population led to high transport costs, and only tariff protection from the 1820s guarded the Urals industries from ruinous competition from English iron. In addition, the timber resources close to the mining centres had been depleted during the rapid period of growth in the eighteenth century, and, as supplies became more distant, costs inevitably rose.

Do the developments that occurred in the Russian economy after the 1830s constitute an industrial revolution? There is evidence enough of a quickening in industrial activity, yet this must be placed in perspective. The iron industry remained backward and, until the very end of the period, stagnant. Coal mining hardly developed at all, and in 1860 only some 18 million poods were mined. Russia relied on imports for nearly all her machinery and railway equipment, and the railway network was only embryonic in 1860. Private banking, too, remained almost entirely undeveloped. Portal [57] has argued convincingly that the advances before 1861 cannot be described as revolutionary; he stresses the narrow range of sectors involved, and the fact that mechanisation made little progress except in cotton textiles and sugar-beet. Cotton textiles were, indeed, with their 'free' labour force, the only 'modern' industry of the type developing in Western Europe. Yet in the Moscow district at the time of the Emancipation, some 350,000 cotton workers were employed on the putting-out system, while only 80,000 were employed in factories. It should be remembered that throughout the first half of the nineteenth century, despite the progress of Russian industry, Russia fell relatively further behind her main competitors, as was clearly seen during the Crimean War (1854-6).

The statistics of industrial workers and of the numbers of manufacturing enterprises look impressive until one recalls the very small establishments that were often included. Such statistics are a poor indication of the rise of modern industry in Russia. The average number of workers in Russia's officially recorded 'factories and plants' was low and showed a tendency to decline towards the end of the period. This may indicate a wider coverage in the collection of statistics, or it may indicate simply the buoyancy of small-scale industry. Certainly, a glance at Table 4 (p. 33 above) will show how very many tiny establishments were included in the data, particularly in the production of commodities such as leather, tallow, soap, candles and wax. The total number of industrial enterprises rose from about 2,400 in 1804 to over 15,000 in 1860; yet a Soviet historian has estimated that the number of these plants employing sixteen or more workers rose only from about 1,200 to 2,818 during the period.

Gerschenkron, looking for a sharp discontinuity in industrial development, argues that the significant phase did not occur until the end of the nineteenth century. Blackwell, however, has recently emphasised the importance of the pre-Reform period as providing a base for Russia's subsequent industrialisation.[11] Certainly, in a number of sectors such a base was laid. Yet, as we shall see, the main characteristics of Russia's later industrialisation – the growth of capital-goods industries and the extension of mining and metallurgy to southern districts – remained largely unheralded before the Emancipation. To repeat what was said in the Introduction: the difference between the Western and Soviet historians considered here is primarily one of emphasis.

[11] See Blackwell [5], and the review of Blackwell's book by Gerschenkron [42].

42

A study of quantitative changes leads to the conclusion that Russia in 1860 was industrially extremely backward, with serfdom providing a major obstacle to further development; that few sectors showed any modern growth; and that despite an obvious increase in economic activity, the main period of industrialisation came considerably later. Qualitatively, however, there were fundamental changes. Mechanised factories made their appearance, and privately-owned factories employing hired labour became a significant element in Russia's industrial structure.

5 Outline of Industrial Development, 1861–1913

THE Emancipation of the Serfs in 1861 removed a considerable barrier to industrial growth. Baykov, however, has suggested that serfdom should not be regarded as the principal obstacle to Russian economic development. He stresses that enough peasants were free of servile status even before the Emancipation to provide a substantial industrial labour force. The presence of serf entrepreneurs and the development of freely hired *obrok* serfs may also warn us against exaggerating the restrictive elements of serfdom. Baykov emphasises rather the 'real' hindrances to Russian industrialisation: the vast distances and harsh climate, and the inaccessibility of much of Russia's mineral wealth prior to the railway age.

On the other hand, serfdom was clearly incompatible with the requirements of an industrialising country. The basis of such a society was agriculture, and serfdom ensured a restricted home market and a low level of agricultural technology. This in turn meant a low level of per capita incomes, which further perpetuated economic backwardness. Serfdom meant too a largely immobile population in which the level of education of the masses was abysmal. The simple pyramid structure of this stratified society, with its huge peasant base and small elite of landed gentry, left little room for the development of a prosperous middle class. As in other backward countries, religious minorities played a part in industrial development out of all proportion to their numbers, with the Old Believers and Jews being particularly important in Russia. Above all, perhaps, serfdom bred values and attitudes inimical to modernisation, and such values were not easily overcome in the post-Emancipation period. Industrialisation, with the prospect of social upheaval that it entailed, was hardly likely to hold much appeal for the landed classes. The greatly unequal distribution of the national income did not lead to the accumulation of savings by the wealthy for industrial development; rather, investment in land and in the acquisition of serfs was preferred. At the same time a high level of consumption of luxury goods (mostly imported) and large expenditures on foreign travel were indulged in by many of the Russian aristocracy. The strong ties of the peasant to the land, too, were an enduring feature of Russian society throughout the nineteenth century. Gerschenkron is surely right to stress the importance of Alexander II's (1855–81) great measure as a stimulus to Russian economic development, and indeed the year 1861 can in many respects be taken as marking the beginning of Russia's modernisation.

With this said, the economic basis built prior to the Emancipation must not be overlooked. We have noticed that, despite the stagnation of heavy industries, there was significant progress in the decades before 1861 in a number of consumer industries. There was, in this respect, continuity across the gulf of the Emancipation. It was in the expansion of heavy industry that the Emancipation can be seen as a decisive turning-point.

Between the Emancipation and the outbreak of the First World War, Russia's industrial structure was transformed. The main feature of this transformation was the growth of heavy industry. Coal and iron mining, metallurgical enterprises, oil production and refining, and several other industries developed rapidly. Consumer-goods industries continued to grow too, although their progress was relatively less marked. Factory production based on the use of steam power steadily eroded the position of handicraft workers, although the workshop industries which did not compete directly with the factories continued to flourish.

With the rise of new industries came the rise of new centres of production. There was rapid development of coal and iron mining and metallurgy in the Ukraine from the 1880s, and the relative importance of the Urals declined. Another new industrial centre emerged in the Caucasus, where the oil industry expanded very rapidly during the 1880s and 1890s.

Goldsmith and Gerschenkron have produced quantitative studies of the overall performance of Tsarist industry after Emancipation.[12] Goldsmith estimated that total industrial pro-

[12] Goldsmith [8] provides aggregate series of agricultural and industrial production; Gerschenkron [30] is concerned with analysing the industrial growth rate.

duction grew by about 5 per cent a year during the period 1860–1913; growth accelerated markedly after the mid-1880s, based primarily on the expansion of heavy industry. Since population growth averaged roughly 1·5 per cent per annum, the annual industrial growth rate was in the region of 3·5 per cent – quite high by comparison with other countries at the time, although it must be remembered that the industrial base from which Russia grew was slender. Agricultural output, however, grew only a little faster than the rate of population increase; since the weight of agriculture in the economy remained high, total real output per head grew slowly, at perhaps 1 per cent annually between 1860 and 1913.

Gerschenkron, basing his study on the index of industrial production compiled by the Russian economist Kondratiev, for the period 1885–1913, has analysed the discontinuous pattern of Russian growth. He calls attention to two periods of very rapid growth in Russian industrialisation. In the 1890s the rate of industrial production exceeded 8 per cent annually, a figure unequalled by any other advanced nation at that period. A further, though quantitatively less spectacular, boom followed after 1907, while the intervening period, between 1900 and 1906, was marked by general stagnation in Russia's industries (see Table 9).

TABLE 9

RATE OF INDUSTRIAL GROWTH IN RUSSIA, 1885–1913

Years	Annual rate (%)
1885–9	6·10
1890–9	8·03
1900–6	1·43
1907–13	6·25
(1910–13	7·50)
1895–1913	5·72

SOURCE: [30] 146.

6 The Emancipation of the Serfs and Economic Development

RUSSIA'S peasant population amounted to some 40 million on the eve of the Emancipation. Of these, a little over half were in personal bondage to the Russian gentry, while the remainder consisted principally of various categories of 'state' and 'crown' peasants. The 1861 Act, together with several other measures affecting Russia's administrative and judicial system, could not fail to influence Russia's economic life, and the year 1861 forms an important landmark in Russian economic history.

Yet while the retarding elements of serfdom on economic development are obvious, Gerschenkron has emphasised also the retarding features of the Reform itself.[13] He points out that under the terms of the Emancipation a prosperous peasant class was not created. In other words, the spur to industrialisation that might have come from the internal demand of a mass market remained lacking. Also, despite the poverty of the peasants, the Emancipation did not stimulate a flow of cheap labour to industrial occupations, and, allied to these points, agricultural productivity failed to show any significant increase, so that the rural sector continued backward and impoverished after 1861.

Under the terms of the Emancipation the peasantry as a whole received insufficient land, less than they had been using on their own account as serfs. Peasant allotments were particularly small in the fertile areas of the black-earth belt and southern steppes. Here the landowners retained as much land for their own use as they could, whereas in the less fertile regions of the centre and north peasant holdings were larger. In all, it appears that the peasantry lost some 4·1 per cent of the land they had used formerly. But this low figure conceals a loss as great as 23·3 per

[13] Gerschenkron [31] is a study of major importance on this subject.

cent in the sixteen black-earth and steppe provinces, and 30·8 per cent in the Ukraine alone.

The peasants were not given their land, but had to pay compensation to the former landowners. For most peasants this meant paying a fixed annual sum to the state, the state in turn compensating the landowners with state bonds. Peasant repayments were to be spread over a period of forty-nine years. These redemption payments were calculated on the value of the land received, and since this valuation was considerably in excess of the true market value, they represented a severe tax burden on the peasantry. Redemption payments, together with numerous other direct and indirect taxes, did much to depress the purchasing power of the peasant subsequent to the Emancipation.

Most peasants did not own their land individually. Over a large part of the country, ownership was vested in the peasant commune (the *obshchina*, or *mir*), an institution which had an ancient tradition in Russia and which was strengthened under the terms of the 1861 Reform. The *mir*, whatever its role in Russian rural society, had a deleterious effect on economic life. The absence of private ownership, and the fact that peasant lands were subject to periodic redistributions among the members of the commune, reduced the incentive for peasants to make long-term improvements in their land and invest capital in their holdings, even if they could afford to do so. At the same time the inefficiencies associated with strip farming, such as the difficulty of introducing new crop rotations, the uneconomic size of strips, and the lengthy journeys a peasant was obliged to make to his scattered holdings, all depressed agricultural productivity. In general, therefore, according to Gerschenkron, poverty in Russia's agricultural sector was built into the terms of the Emancipation, and hindered the development of the internal market in the second half of the nineteenth century.

It should be pointed out, however, that, onerous as the Emancipation terms undoubtedly were, they did not necessarily mean an overall diminution of peasant purchasing power. As the economy developed, especially with the building of the railways and growing urbanisation, it was possible for peasants to market their crops where previously these had sometimes remained

48

unharvested because of the lack of a market. Moreover, the redemption payments were often no higher than the rents paid by former serfs.

Contemporaries became increasingly aware of the 'agricultural problem' as the century progressed, for the problem itself became more severe. If the peasants had received inadequate land at the time of the Emancipation, the rapid expansion of population thereafter, allied to the continued low level of productivity, ensured that the insufficiency would become worse. Lyashchenko estimated that about one-quarter of the peasants received land allotments inadequate to support themselves at the time of the Emancipation. By 1910 the proportion had risen to over a half. Rural overpopulation was naturally most severe in those regions where the 1861 settlement had been most inadequate, and where opportunities for alternative industrial employment were small. The central agricultural regions were especially badly hit, and acute distress followed the not infrequent harvest failures. 'Land hunger' manifested itself in steady purchases of land by peasant communes from the gentry estates, which usually entailed mounting peasant indebtedness. Despite the low levels of agricultural productivity and the general fall in agricultural prices, land prices rose steadily after 1861. At the same time, the growth of the rural population meant that the average landholding of the peasants declined throughout the post-Emancipation period (see Table 10).

Movement off the land to the urban centres was not possible on a large enough scale (and emigration to the empty lands of Siberia did not become a serious possibility until the very end

TABLE 10

AVERAGE PEASANT HOLDINGS, 1860–90
(dessyatins*)

	1860	1880	1890
Northern Region	7·6	6·1	4·7
Central Agricultural Region	3·6	2·5	2·0
South-west	2·9	2·1	1·4
Ukraine	3·3	2·5	1·7

SOURCE: [3] 179.

* 1 dessyatin = approx. 2·7 acres (1·1 hectares).

49

of the century). Partly this was simply because the rate of industrial growth in Russia was too low to absorb the surplus rural population; partly the problem can again be traced to the strengthening of the *mir* under the terms of the Emancipation. Peasants were frequently tied to their commune. If they wished to leave they had to purchase a passport, and none the less often remained liable for their share of communal taxes (for taxes were levied not on individuals but on the commune as a whole). Thus, the flow of labour to industrial centres was restricted, and Gerschenkron considers this a further retarding feature of the Emancipation.

Gerschenkron rightly emphasises these retarding elements in the Reform, but some of his arguments are open to misunderstanding. 'It would be surprising indeed if an existing demand for industrial labour was not met by supply in a backward rural country like Russia, and there is little evidence that the formal commune regulations restricted the labour supply in this manner. Passports to enable members to work away from the commune were issued in substantial numbers, and it is reasonable to suppose that had demand existed, mobility from village to town would have increased accordingly. Under the terms of the Emancipation a large number of Russians had no land at all and could in theory have supplied a factory labour force. This number may have amounted to between 2 and 3 million – far more than the total factory work-force in 1861, and possibly as high as that which existed at the end of the boom of the 1890s. There were, it is true, complaints of labour shortages by industrialists, but such complaints came in the main from the newly industrialising southern regions, where population was relatively sparse, where agriculture was developing in response to the growth of export markets and hence competed with industry for labour, and where in any case the commune was frequently not well established. Labour shortages occurred most often at harvest time, when workers were often in the habit of leaving their industrial employment. Thus, the slow growth of an industrial labour force can be attributed only in part to an inelastic supply; it was due also to the nature of the Russian economy, in particular to the slow growth of opportunities for industrial employment.

50

7 Industrial Growth before the 1890s

ALTHOUGH Russian industry continued to exhibit many features of a backward, agrarian-based structure in the decades after the Emancipation, definite growth did take place. Goldsmith's figures show that in aggregate terms industry grew only slowly in the 1860s and 1870s, but from the middle of the 1880s a significant upturn occurred. A few statistics will illustrate this development. The labour force in the industries covered by official data, including railways, approximately doubled in the thirty years after 1860, so that by 1890 the number of workers stood at 1,433,000. Production in numerous industrial sectors mounted impressively. Coal output was some 18·3 million poods in 1860, and by 1890 had reached 367·2 million poods (see Table 11). Over the same period, iron and

TABLE 11

COAL PRODUCTION, 1860–1913
(million poods)

1860–4	21·8	1890–4	434·3
1865–9	28·4	1895–9	673·3
1870–4	61·9	1900–4	1,057·7
1875–9	131·3	1905–9	1,444·5
1880–4	225·4	1910–13	1,840·2
1885–9	302·6		

SOURCE: [13] 453–4.

steel production rose from 12·4 to 48·4 million poods, iron ore from 45·9 to 106·3 million poods. Before the 1870s petroleum production was negligible, but between 1883 and 1890 output grew from 60·4 million poods to 241·9 million poods. The transport network made considerable progress, especially the construction of railways. In 1860 Russia possessed a mere 1,626 km. of track, but by 1890 the network had expanded to 30,596 km. Consumer-goods industries also showed development, and the consumption of raw cotton grew from 2·8 to 8·3 million poods between 1860 and 1890 (see Table 12).

TABLE 12

COTTON CONSUMPTION, 1865–1913
(million poods)

1865–9	2·7	1890–4	10·1
1870–4	3·7	1895–9	14·0
1875–9	5·6	1900–4	16·7
1880–4	7·8	1905–9	19·7
1885–9	9·2	1910–13	23·8

SOURCE: [13] 453–4.

The first half of the 1860s were years of considerable difficulty for Russian industry, and many branches showed declining production. There were two major problems. The first was the aftermath of the Emancipation and the needs of Russian industries to adapt to the new conditions. Most vulnerable were those enterprises which had relied on bonded labour – the possessional factories of the Urals, and the *votchinal* enterprises on the great estates. Mining and metallurgy, woollen textiles, sugar and paper production were adversely affected. From 20·5 million poods in 1860, pig-iron production slumped to 15·3 million poods in 1862, and not until 1870 did output once more exceed the 1860 level (see Table 13). In the great Demidov enterprises in the Urals, the flight of former serfs reduced the work-force from 25,585 to 9,147 by 1862. Output of refined

TABLE 13

PIG-IRON PRODUCTION, 1860–1913
(million poods)

1860–4	18·1	1890–4	66·9
1865–9	18·9	1895–9	120·9
1870–4	22·9	1900–4	169·0
1875–9	25·9	1905–9	170·8
1880–4	29·2	1910–13	236·1
1885–9	37·6		

SOURCE: [13] 453–4.

sugar fell from 3·4 million poods in 1860 to 1·9 million in 1863, although thereafter it rose substantially. The number of woollen-textile workers declined from 99,000 to 71,800 between 1859 and 1863, and the value of paper production fell from 49·8 million roubles in 1861 to 38·7 million roubles in 1863.

The second major problem of the 1860s, and one which makes it difficult to estimate the impact of the Emancipation, was the 'cotton famine' which occurred during the American Civil War. Cotton textiles, the largest industry in the country, relied entirely on imports of raw cotton, mostly from the United States. Cotton consumption fell from 2,840,000 poods in 1860 to only 850,000 poods in 1862, and the slump had repercussions on the rest of the economy.

By the late 1860s, however, expansion was under way in most branches of the economy, and by the 1880s the economy was set for a period of rapid progress. The pace of Russian industrialisation was by no means even, however.[14] The late 1860s and early 1870s saw a considerable boom. The value of output of thirty-four leading industries, according to Lenin's data, rose from 235·8 million roubles in 1867 to 352·1 million roubles in 1872, an increase of 49 per cent, while employment rose by 27 per cent. Another indication of the greater pace of economic activity was an increase in the number of joint-stock companies established. Between 1861 and 1865, 44 such companies were established with a total nominal capital of 99 million roubles. In the years 1869–73, however, no fewer than 281 were established with a capital of 697 million roubles. In the four years 1868–71, 8,603 km. of railways were opened to traffic, whereas the entire network in 1867 was only 5,038 km. Internal trade flourished also, sales at the Nizhni-Novgorod fair yielding 110·2 million silver roubles in 1868 and 154·3 million in 1872.

This rather frenzied boom gave way to a severe depression in 1873, but by the end of the 1870s revival was once more under way, stimulated in part by war-time demands during the Turkish conflict of 1877–8. A series of excellent harvests, which led to record grain exports in 1878 and 1879, also stimulated pros-

[14] Yakovlev [16] provides a detailed analysis of cyclical fluctuations in Russia during the nineteenth century.

perity. A further sharp crisis in 1882 was succeeded by an upturn in the second half of the 1880s. In 1890 came a further recession in most sectors of the economy, and this slump was deepened by a catastrophic harvest failure and subsequent widespread famine in 1891.

It will be noticed that the general course of the ebbs and flows in Russian economic activity followed a pattern very similar to that of the international economic cycle. There is no doubt that by the second half of the nineteenth century the commercial and financial links of Russia with other nations had brought much of her economy to a position of interdependence with them. As mentioned earlier, Strumilin's researches have shown Russia's participation in the international trade cycle to extend back well before the Emancipation. At the same time, however, internal considerations also played an important part in determining the course of activity in Russia. As Yakovlev has shown, the state of the harvest and level of agricultural prices were a major influence throughout, affecting as they did both the extent of home demand and the level of government revenue.

Beyond the factors influencing the cyclical behaviour of the Russian economy were factors making for long-term growth. From the late 1860s railway construction was a dominant force in Russia's industrial development, while in the 1880s the development of tariff protection provided another powerful influence. Before the Emancipation few railway lines of economic significance had been constructed. Following 1861, however, the railways had a growing impact on Russian industrialisation. In 1874 the railway network stood at 18,220 km. and by 1890 a further 12,376 km. had been added (see Table 14). During the 1860s several important lines were built to serve the central industrial regions, such as the Moscow–Kursk, Moscow–Voronezh and Moscow–Nizhi-Novgorod lines. In this and the subsequent decade railways were also constructed in the grain-producing regions of the south, and the Kursk–Kharkov–Odessa and Kharkov–Rostov lines linked the principal agricultural regions to the Black Sea ports. Railway construction expanded too in the Baltic regions, in the Urals and in the Polish provinces. The 1880s saw a general slackening in con-

TABLE 14

ANNUAL AVERAGE RAILWAY CONSTRUCTION, 1861–1913

Year	km.	Year	km.
1861–5	443	1891–5	1,292
1866–70	1,378	1896–1900	3,235
1871–5	1,660	1901–5	1,570
1876–80	767	1906–10	1,099
1881–5	632	1911–13	1,192
1886–90	914		

SOURCE: [13] 462.

struction, but some lines of considerable economic importance were built. The Ekaterine railway, opened in 1885, linked the coal regions of the Donetz Basin with the iron ore of Krivoi Rog in the Ukraine. In the Caucasus, the Baku–Batum railway, opened in 1883, joined the main producing regions on the Caspian to the Black Sea, and thus opened the way for a spectacular growth of Russian oil exports.

Enough has been said about the obstacles placed in the path of Russian economic development by factors such as distance and climate to make the importance of the railways evident. In addition to providing a form of freight and passenger transport vastly more reliable and speedy than existing facilities, they also directly fostered native industry by their demands for materials and by their employment of many thousands of workers in construction and operation. The total numbers employed by the railway companies grew from some 32,000 in 1865 to 252,000 by 1890.

Until 1880 most of Russia's railways were built and operated by private companies, although usually these benefited from state encouragement in the form of guarantees and subsidies. Between 1861 and 1880 more than four-fifths of the network was constructed privately. After 1880, however, the Government began to play a more active role. The state directly constructed and operated the majority of new lines, started to buy out existing companies, and kept a strict control over the policies of such private companies as remained. By the outbreak of the First World War more than two-thirds of the entire network was owned and operated by the state.

55

Relatively low tariffs prevailed in Russia between the 1850s and the 1870s, and major liberal tariff measures came into force in 1857 and 1868. During the period of low tariffs imports rose substantially, and despite an expansion of agricultural exports, Russia had a trade deficit throughout the 1860s and 1870s. Many of Russia's industries were encouraged by low import duties. The railway companies benefited from cheap imports of rails and locomotives (mostly from Britain), since Russia's own industries could provide no more than a small fraction of their requirements. Between 1866 and 1875 alone, imports of iron rails and locomotives amounted to over 1,000 million roubles. Most of Russia's coal was imported also. The St Petersburg industries, for example, found it cheaper to buy coal from Britain than from Poland or the Ukraine. In general, low tariffs stimulated the development of light industries, especially those with easy access to the ports. The cotton-textile mills, for example, relied on foreign supplies of raw cotton and on imports of machinery. Not surprisingly, however, Russia's capital-goods industries, which found foreign competition severe, did not make substantial progress. The state endeavoured at times to foster these industries. In 1876 railway companies were obliged to purchase half their rails from Russian manufacturers, while concessions and subsidies were given at times to domestic and foreign industrialists. But the rapid growth of Russia's heavy industries did not come until the middle of the 1880s.

From what has been said, it is apparent that before the 1880s the Russian Government did not play a direct role in much of the industrial expansion that occurred. Encouragement given by the state to private railway companies, however, did provide an important expansionary force. Liberal tariffs, too, encouraged private investment in several industrial sectors. There was also an undoubted increase in domestic demand. The need for cash by the peasants in order to meet their tax obligations stimulated the growth of commercial agriculture and the spread of a money economy. Agricultural output grew, due mainly to the extension of cultivation. The principal stimulus came from export demand for wheat, and between the 1870s and the 1890s an increasing proportion of the harvest was sent to foreign markets. Production of grains grew particularly rapidly in the regions serving the ports on the Black Sea and the Sea of Azov. From the 1880s, however, Russian producers suffered from the world-wide recession in agricultural prices, and for the next two decades the expansion of grain sales did not bring corresponding gains in income.

From the 1880s the state came to play a more active role in the economy. Increasingly, the Government became concerned with the balance of trade and with the strength of the rouble, and this led successive Ministers of Finance to take budgetary measures which influenced the direction of economic development. In these years foreign investment in Russia began to mount, and this raised the problem of acquiring foreign currency to service the debt. At the same time there was a growing uneasiness at Russia's evident backwardness compared with the other great powers. It was partly for strategic reasons that the state directly undertook the construction of railways after 1880.

The ending of liberal tariffs came in 1877. In that year the duties that existed were increased by about one-third, although the tariff structure which permitted free or nearly free importation of raw material and semi-manufactured commodities remained unchanged. In the decade following, however, the level of protection was increased considerably. There were major Tariff Acts in 1881 and 1882, and these were supplemented in the succeeding years, culminating in the 'monster' tariff of 1891. The growing level of tariff protection is indicated by the increase in tariff revenue as a proportion of the total value of imports. This rose from 12·8 per cent in the years 1869–76 to an average of 28·3 per cent in 1885–90 and to 33 per cent during the 1890s (see Table 15).

The era of protection stimulated the rapid development of such industries as iron and coal mining, metallurgy, oil production and machine construction. From the 1880s, therefore, Russia acquired the beginnings of a substantial heavy industrial sector.

The main centres of heavy industry were developed in the Ukraine, although in absolute terms it was not until the 1890s that the southern regions overtook the Urals in iron production. In 1890, of a total production of pig-iron of 56·6 million poods, the Urals accounted for 24·0 million, the south for 13·4 million.

57

TABLE 15

TARIFF LEVELS, 1868 AND 1891
(gold kopeks per pood)

Commodity	1868 tariff	1891 tariff
Coal	Free	2–3
Iron ore	Free	10·5
Pig-iron	5	45–52·5
Cast iron	50–250	112·5–255
Steel	20–50	90–150
Rails	20	90
Industrial machinery	30	250
Steam engines	75	300
Locomotives	30	170
Agricultural machinery	Free	70–140
Raw cotton	Free	120–135
Cotton yarn	325	420–540
Cotton goods	28–110	32–135

SOURCE: [1] II 199.

The southern works, however, were considerably more productive, using modern technology and operating on a larger scale. The south had 22 iron mines in operation in 1890 whereas the Urals possessed 435; yet the total labour force in the iron mines and metallurgical works in the south was 15,698, while in the Urals it totalled 165,057.

The Ukrainian iron industry dates effectively from 1869, although long before that time numerous unsuccessful attempts had been made to found metallurgical enterprises there. In 1869 a British ironfounder, John Hughes, contracted with the Russian Government to establish an ironworks near Lugansk, in the Donetz region. Hughes received government orders for iron rails on very favourable terms, and soon the success of his enterprise attracted other foreign capitalists as well as Russian entrepreneurs. The discovery of coal in the Lugansk area in 1873, and of very rich iron deposits in the Krivoi Rog region in 1882, opened the way for the development of heavy industry in the Ukraine.

Simultaneously with the development of the iron industry came the expansion of coal. Here too foreign capital played an important initiating role. As with iron, the existence of coal had long been known in the Donetz Basin, but not until the era of railway building did output rise significantly. The Kursk–Kharkov–Azov railway, opened in 1869, tapped some of the richest coal regions in the western Donetz. Coal could now be sent by rail to the interior of Russia, while the Lozovo–Sevastopol line (1873) and the Kharkov–Nikolaiev (1870–8) linked the Donetz mines with the Black Sea ports. In 1870 only 2·6 million poods of bituminous coal were produced in the Donetz region. By 1880 output was 57·1 million and, stimulated by tariff protection in 1884, reached 146·8 million poods by 1890. Railways not only carried Donetz coal to markets; they were also the leading consumers of coal for most of the 1880s. The other major markets for coal were provided by the growing southern industries, principally metallurgy and also sugar-beet. Thus the development of the coal industry was closely linked with the industrialisation of southern Russia.

Russia's oil industry was centred in the Caucasus, where the Baku region, on the Caspian Sea, accounted for more than 90 per cent of total output throughout the period. The familiar problems of inadequate capital supplies and remoteness of markets had long held back the development of Russia's rich oil resources. But in the 1870s the base was laid for what became in the 1880s Russia's fastest-growing industry. Foreign capital was poured into refining and, to a lesser extent, production. In 1874 the Nobel brothers began their famous enterprise, incorporated in 1878 as the Nobel Brothers Naphtha Company, and during the 1880s another giant concern was started by the French Rothschilds. The Nobels built the world's first oil-tankers, which carried their oil on the Caspian Sea to Astrakhan whence it was distributed via the Volga and rail to the internal markets of Russia. At this time oil (kerosene) was used primarily for lighting purposes and rapidly became a necessity even for the poorest peasant. The disruption of United States supplies during the Turkish War enabled the Russian industry to capture a mass home market in the southern provinces of the country, and tariff protection soon secured the entire domestic market for Russian producers (see Table 16). Imports became negligible, and with the construction of the rail link to Batum (acquired as a result of the Turkish War) in 1883, Russia soon became a major competitor with the United States on world markets.

TABLE 16

RUSSIAN OIL PRODUCTION, 1885–1913
(million poods)

1885–9	153·4	1900–4	658·9
1890–4	281·8	1905–9	512·6
1895–9	456·9	1910–13	569·4

Source: [13] 459.

We can see, therefore, that import substitution played a significant part in Russia's industrialisation in the latter part of the nineteenth century. This was aided by transport developments, which linked distant centres of production with internal markets, as well as by the high level of tariff protection. Domestic sources of capital investment, extremely scarce in such a backward country as Russia, were supplemented by foreign investment. Such investment was often, as in the case of the oil industry in the Caucasus, accompanied by foreign skills and technology, and by foreign managers and even skilled artisans.

8   The Boom of the 1890s

DURING the decade of the 1890s Russian industry made impressive advances. To a large extent, the Russian economy moved in this decade further along the path already in evidence during the 1880s, and many writers have dated Russia's 'take-off' from the middle of the 1880s.

According to Gerschenkron, the most significant factor in Russia's industrial upsurge in the 1890s was the role played by the state. Government policy conditioned the industrial structure that emerged in Russia; it dictated, for example, that capital-goods industries rather than consumer goods should develop most rapidly, and that foreign capital should play an increasingly important part in the development of Russian industry.

The industrial boom of the 1890s is closely linked with the policies of the powerful and able Minister of Finance, Sergei Witte, whose tenure at the ministry lasted from 1893 to 1903. As von Laue and others have shown (see, for example, [73]), Witte made the industrialisation of Russia a prime objective, and his policies in these years are sometimes referred to as the 'Witte system'. There are dangers, however, in using such a phrase without qualification. While it is true that Witte was an ardent advocate of industrialisation, and pursued his aims with a vigour lacking in his predecessors, it is true also that there were elements of inconsistency and expedience in his economic policies. Fortune played its part too. The influx of foreign capital in the 1890s, for example, was certainly encouraged by Witte's financial policies, but it was encouraged also by the very low international interest rates in the period and by the favourable publicity given to Russia's industrial prospects in France, Russia's new-found ally.

Under Witte's guidance the Ministry of Finance became an instrument for promoting rapid industrial development in Russia. Budget revenues were approximately doubled in the 1890s, and the state poured funds into a wide variety of economic projects, above all the railways, and encouraged others. To a large extent Witte's motives were political, and this in turn influenced the nature of Russia's industrialisation. Russia was easily the most backward of the world's great powers. Despite many features of modernisation since the Crimean War – the Emancipation of the Serfs, and the construction of railways, for example – Russia remained economically, and therefore militarily, weak in an environment of increasingly powerful competitors. When Russia and Germany became estranged after 1878, Russia's precarious position was obvious. To Witte, therefore, industrialisation was a race against time; economic strength had to be built rapidly in order that Russia might maintain her position as a great power.

The basis of the industrial strength desired by Witte was the rapid development of the railway network and the expansion of heavy industry. The means by which this end was achieved, the so-called 'system', incorporated tariff protection, monetary stability and financial reform, heavy taxation, and the encouragement of foreign investment. Briefly, the system sprang from Russia's shortage of domestic capital. Taxation of the Russian population could yield funds for government investment, while large domestic loans were also floated. But foreign investment was needed too. If foreigners were to invest sufficiently in Russian securities, the inherent strength of Russia's economy must be shown by a stable rouble and, in the circumstances of the late nineteenth-century international economy, the adoption of the gold standard (which was ultimately achieved in 1897). In turn, this meant the accumulation of large gold reserves and the maintenance of a favourable balance of trade.

Witte preserved the favourable balance of trade secured in the 1880s by continuing a highly protective tariff policy (see Table 17). At the same time, import substitution was encouraged by direct government support of Russian industry. Witte used such methods as generous state contracts and the regulation of railway freight charges, in addition to state investment in the Russian economy. The success of Witte's policy in this direction is shown, for example, by the fact that during the 1870s Russian production of pig-iron had satisfied only two-fifths of domestic consumption, whereas in the 1890s domestic supplies provided some three-quarters of consumption. Yet despite the protective tariffs and the general development of Russia's industries, the level of imports continued to rise during the 1890s. Partly this is explained, of course, by industrialisation

TABLE 17

RUSSIAN FOREIGN TRADE, 1861–1913
(million roubles)

Year	Exports	Imports	Balance
1861–70	222·7	225·9	− 3·2
1871–80	454·8	488·2	− 33·4
1881–90	622·2	471·8	+150·4.
1891–1900	659·8	535·4	+124·4
1901–10	1,073·1	887·4	+185·7

SOURCE: [26] 301.

itself, which brought with it a demand for many raw materials, machinery and other products which Russia could not produce herself.

The state also took measures to stimulate agricultural exports and thereby to preserve a favourable balance of trade. The construction of railways in the regions supplying the export markets led to an expansion of foreign sales. At the same time, von Laue suggests that heavy taxation of the peasantry – purposely levied after the harvest when prices were lowest – forced the sale of agricultural products. Taxation thus served a dual purpose. It provided funds for state investment, and it also fostered exports at a time of falling world prices of food products. Thus the government budgetary policy 'squeezed' an agricultural surplus from the Russian peasantry.

Gerschenkron views the predominant role of the state in the process of industrialisation largely as a response to conditions of economic backwardness. The state, as it were, compensated through budgetary policies for the domestic demand and indigenous supplies of private capital which were lacking in Russia. Yet these budgetary policies limited still further the possibility of a mass domestic market arising in Russia. Witte himself was well aware of the dilemma presented by the agrarian situation, but he hoped that successful industrialisation would ultimately produce prosperity in Russia in which agriculture would share.

Von Laue possibly exaggerates the extent of the 'changed direction' of the 1890s. To some extent, most of the features of Witte's system were present in earlier decades. Under three powerful Ministers of Finance, Reutern (1862–76), Bunge (1881–6) and Vishnegradski (1887–92), numerous measures had been undertaken to improve state finances, stabilise the rouble and encourage the flow of foreign capital. Under Vishnegradski the burden of indirect taxation increased, with a substantial part of government revenue coming from duties on articles of mass consumption, such as vodka, kerosene and sugar. Again, as we have seen, tariff protection became a significant element in Russian industrialisation in the 1880s, and it was Vishnegradski's tariff of 1891 which, with few modifications, remained the basis of Russia's tariff structure throughout the 1890s and until 1914. By such measures a favourable balance of trade had been achieved during the 1880s and, indeed, the surplus declined somewhat in the following decade as industrialisation led to increased imports.

Certainly, Witte pursued industrialisation with a singleness of purpose lacking in his predecessors. In those years state activity had promoted industrial growth as a by-product of its railway policy. Witte's main weapon was also railway construction, but he used his railway policies as part of a far more vigorous industrialisation drive than did his predecessors. However, to a large extent Witte's policies were a continuation of earlier policies, and their success was dependent on the groundwork already established.

In the 1890s, then, Russian industrialisation made rapid progress. The annual industrial growth rate of slightly more than 8 per cent was certainly an impressive achievement. The basis of this growth was the expansion of heavy industry, particularly in the Ukraine. The industrial census of 1897 provided reasonably reliable figures for factory enterprises (excluding, that is, *kustar* and small-scale artisan industries) for the years 1887 and 1897 (see Table 18). The census demonstrated the advances made during the 1890s. The value of output of all industry more than doubled in ten years, while the total industrial labour force, including railway workers, was approaching 3 million by the end of the 1890s. Neither the value of output nor employment can be considered entirely satisfactory measures of development. Price changes were not uniform. Heavy tariff duties meant that for many industrial products Russian prices

TABLE 18

RUSSIAN INDUSTRY, 1887 AND 1897

Commodity	Value of production ('000 roubles)		Employment	
	1887	1897	1887	1897
Textiles	463,044	946,296	399,178	642,520
Food products	375,286	648,116	205,223	255,357
Animal products	79,495	132,058	38,876	64,418
Wood products	25,688	102,897	30,703	86,273
Paper	21,030	45,490	19,491	46,190
Chemicals	21,509	59,555	21,134	35,320
Ceramics	28,965	82,590	67,346	143,291
Mining and metallurgy	156,012	393,749	390,915	544,333
Metal products	112,618	310,626	103,300	214,311
Others	50,852	117,767	41,882	66,249
Total	1,334,499	2,839,144	1,318,048	2,098,262

SOURCE: [27] 291.

rose at a time when world prices were moving in the opposite direction. Again, increases in productivity, especially in mining and metallurgy, make the growth of employment a doubtful indicator. At the same time, the spectacular increases shown by the census in such industries as wood products, paper, ceramics and metal-working reflect to some extent the growth of factory enterprise in these fields at the expense of workshop production.

Railway construction dominated the industrial upsurge of the 1890s. Between 1890 and 1900 the length of track expanded from 30,596 km. to 53,234 km. The last three years of the decade saw an annual average of 3,883 km. opened, more than double the average of the 1867–75 boom. The major part in this burst of construction was taken by the Government, and state railway investment (including guaranteed loans) amounted in all to some 3,500 million roubles during the decade. The rail network in European Russia was considerably enlarged and improved in these years, and important new lines were built in the Urals, the Lower Volga area and the Caucasus. But the most ambitious undertakings were state-financed projects in the Asiatic provinces, above all the Trans-Siberian railway, begun in 1891 and completed a decade later. Moscow and St Petersburg were linked by rail with Vladivostok on the Pacific coast, and the economic exploitation of new territories commenced. During the 1890s large-scale emigration to Western Siberia got under way, and the development of cotton growing in Turkestan provided a new source of raw material for the textile industries; by 1913 more than half of Russia's cotton consumption was produced domestically.

In 1890 Russia had ranked fifth among nations in terms of rail network. By 1900 she was in second place · to the United States. Relative to her vast area, of course, Russia's network remained thin and inadequate, yet in absolute terms it represented an enormous industry. Railway construction greatly stimulated industrialisation by its demands for capital equipment. The Ukrainian industries especially felt the effects of this demand. During the 1890s probably more than one-third of Russian iron output was taken directly by the railway industry, while railways also stimulated the establishment of large locomotive works. The railways, too, continued to provide a major market for Russian coal.

Textiles remained far and away the leading industry in the 1890s. During the decade mechanisation became dominant in all sectors of industry, while a very considerable expansion of cotton textiles took place in the provinces of Moscow and Vladimir. Yet the weight of heavy industry in the economy increased considerably. The annual rates of growth of the value of output among the various sectors of the economy were as follows: mining, 11·2 per cent; chemicals, 10·7 per cent; lumber, 9·3 per cent; metallurgy, 8·4 per cent; ceramics, 8·0 per cent; textiles, 7·8 per cent; and food processing, 1·7 per cent.

Those factors which had stimulated the growth of heavy industry in the 1880s – the growth of railway construction, tariff protection, direct government investment and the influx of foreign capital – continued on a greatly enhanced scale to foster the development of heavy industry in the 1890s. Total coal production grew from 367·2 million poods in 1890 to 995·2 million poods in 1900, while iron-ore output grew over the period from 106·3 million poods to 367·2 million poods. In this decade petroleum output grew from 241 million poods to 632 million poods, and by 1900 Russia was the world's largest oil producer (a situation which did not last more than a couple of years, however). Geographical concentration of industrial production continued along the lines already evident in the 1880s. In 1890 the Donetz Basin produced one-half of Russia's coal output, while in 1900 the proportion had reached nearly 70 per cent. Similarly, the southern iron-ore fields accounted for 57·1 per cent of output in 1900 compared with 21·6 per cent at the beginning of the decade. The southern metallurgical industries grew very rapidly. In 1890 there were only five such enterprises in the Donetz region with an estimated total capital of 13·7 million roubles. In 1895 the number of firms was nine, with a total investment of some 38 million roubles, and by 1900 twenty-one firms had a combined investment of some 144 million roubles.

Soviet writers lay considerable emphasis on the uneven development of Russian industry between the various sectors. Investment in the 'means of production' provides a yardstick by which to measure the stage reached by the development of capitalism. Such investment encouraged the adoption of new techniques and methods of industrial organisation, while at the same time the mobilisation of long-term capital for such enterprises brought important institutional changes such as the development of investment banking. The increasing significance of heavy industry as a whole can be seen from the calculations of Yakovlev. He showed that from an approximate ratio of 30:70 between the value of production in 'heavy' and 'light' industry in 1887, the proportions had changed to 46·5:53·5 in 1900.

Accompanying the industrial upsurge of the 1890s went a tendency towards concentration in large units of production. The numbers of very large enterprises grew rapidly, and they accounted for an increasing share of total industrial output and of the total industrial labour force. By 1900 Russian industry was more highly concentrated in this respect than that of either the

United States or Germany. Large enterprises had long been a feature of Russian industry, and concentration had increased after the Emancipation. During the 1890s, however, the process gathered pace. In 1880 roughly one-third of all Russia's industrial labour force in those enterprises which employed more than 100 workers were to be found in enterprises employing more than 1,000. By 1890 the proportion was nearly two-fifths, and by 1902 it had reached one-half. Concentration was highest in the mining and metallurgical industries of the Ukraine and in the Baku oil industry. By the end of the 1890s, 4 per cent of Russia's coal mines produced some 43 per cent of total output, while 10 per cent of firms in the oil industry accounted for about 70 per cent of total oil production. There was a similar process of concentration in consumer-goods industries, in sugar-beet and textiles for example. In 1880 roughly half the output of cotton textiles was produced in enterprises employing over 100 workers; by 1894 the proportion had risen to nearly three-quarters.

These characteristic features of Russian industrialisation – the increasing importance of capital-goods industries and the growth of large-scale units of production – play an important part in Marxist historical analysis. They have also been discussed by Gerschenkron in terms of his study of the impact of Russia's relative backwardness on industrialisation. The backward Russian economy required huge investment in developing the infrastructure necessary for rapid industrialisation to take place. Above all, this meant the construction of railways. In addition, the particular objectives of the Tsarist Government in the late nineteenth century, especially the construction of railways and the development of an industrial base appropriate to the status of a great power, necessitated an emphasis on capital-goods industries.

Gerschenkron also relates industrial concentration to Russian backwardness. He argues that the relative scarcity of management skills and capital encouraged large units of production. Managerial talent could be used to maximum efficiency in big concerns, while the adoption of advanced technology, given the low level of efficiency of Russian labour, was an economically rational response on the part of Russian industrialists. Greater plant size was certainly encouraged by mechanisation and the growth of capital investment, and also by the rapid growth of corporate business organisation which took place during the 1890s. Yet, while it is true that advanced technology and bigness of scale was a feature of much of Russian industry – for example in the St Petersburg cotton mills and in the metallurgical enterprises of the Ukraine – it is also true that many industrial processes remained primitive and highly labour-intensive. Thus the coal mines of the Donetz Basin used little cutting machinery, and many mines relied on manual labour for surface transportation. Russian labour was notoriously inefficient, and low labour productivity often necessitated a large work-force. Thus the bigness of plant, measured by the number of workers, was often an indication of technological backwardness rather than of a modern, technically advanced, industrial enclave.

Coexisting with big enterprises were large numbers of small-scale establishments. Many of the peasant and artisan industries escaped the net of official statistics, which, in consequence, under-estimate the importance of small-scale industry. Such enterprises were not growing as rapidly as large industries, and where they faced competition from the factories they were often in decline by the close of the nineteenth century. Yet they displayed a remarkable vigour, and Strumilin has estimated that between the 1880s and the end of the 1890s the value of their production may have doubled (compared with a threefold increase in 'large-scale' manufacturing). Russia thus possessed a dual industrial structure, stemming in large measure from her continued economic backwardness, showing the existence of both a high level of industrial concentration in large plants and also a sizeable sector of very small enterprises.

The important part played by foreign capital in Russia's industrialisation has been mentioned earlier, and the encouragement of such investment formed a major element of Tsarist economic policy. Prior to 1914 Russia was Europe's largest debtor nation. A substantial portion of Russia's national debt was held abroad. In 1895, of a total debt of some 5,775 million roubles, about 30 per cent was held by foreigners; by 1914 the national debt had risen to 8,811 million roubles, and the foreign share to 48 per cent. Possibly one-half of this foreign

69

investment was accounted for by state railway loans. Foreign capital also flowed into Russian industries, banks, commercial undertakings and other fields of enterprise. Since a substantial part of the state debt was contracted for industrial projects (especially railways), it is clear that foreign capital must have made an important contribution to Russian industrial development.

No recent study has attempted to quantify the overall totals of foreign capital in Russia. The estimates of Ol', made fifty years ago, still form the basis of most studies of the subject. According to Yatsunsky [9], however, these estimates may exaggerate somewhat the importance of foreign capital investment.

Foreign capital had long participated in Russian economic activity. Even in 1890 between one-quarter and one-third of all investment in Russian joint-stock companies was held abroad. But it was in the decade of the 1890s that the flow of capital rose substantially. According to Ol', foreigners had invested some 214·7 million roubles in Russian enterprises by 1890. In 1895 the total stood at 280·1 million roubles, and thereafter came a huge increase. By 1900 the total had reached 911·0 million roubles, representing roughly one-half of joint-stock company investment in Russia. At this stage there were 269 foreign companies operating in Russia, all but twelve having been founded since 1888. Foreign capital continued to flow into Russia after a lull following the 1900–6 crisis. Between 1906 and 1914 the volume of foreign investment doubled, and by the outbreak of the First World War some 2,000 million roubles of foreign capital had been invested in Russia.

Foreign investment was important not simply for its volume. A large share of investment was concentrated in those industries which provided the spearhead of Russia's industrialisation. Heavy industries in particular attracted a large proportion of foreign capital. Other sectors, such as textiles and food processing, received much less. Roughly half of the total foreign investment in Russian enterprises during the 1890s went into the southern mining and metallurgical industries, and foreign capital may have accounted for nearly 90 per cent of total capital investment in this sector in 1900. Foreign concerns also dominated the oil industry in the Caucasus, and foreign capital provided roughly one-half of investment in machine production in 1900. Even in 1914 foreign capital still provided about 90 per cent of mining investment and over 40 per cent of that in metallurgy. Foreign interests also predominated in many of the major banking concerns. Since the banks in turn played a significant role in the finance of industry and transport, especially after 1907, the vital part played by foreign capital in Russia's industrial expansion cannot be doubted (see Table 19).

France and Belgium (whose industrial and financial institutions had close links with each other) provided the bulk of foreign investment after 1890. French and Belgian capital combined grew from about 33 million roubles in 1880 to 91·2 million roubles in 1890 and to 521·6 million by 1900. In 1917, of a total foreign investment of 2,243 million roubles, according to Ol', France accounted for about 33 per cent, Great Britain 23 per cent, Germany 20 per cent, Belgium 14 per cent and the United States 5 per cent. Most French and Belgian capital was concentrated in the mining and metallurgical industries and in banking. In 1916 nearly two-thirds of all French capital in Russian joint-stock enterprises was in mining and metallurgy and, according to Dr Crisp, the French held nearly 23 per cent of the capital of Russia's ten largest commercial banks. British capital was particularly important in the Russian oil industry and also in cotton textiles and copper production.

What accounts for the rapid inflow of capital into Russia? The view found in some Soviet studies, that the advanced European nations, having reached their imperialist stage, were capturing 'colonial' Russia's industries, is not very helpful. There is no evidence that Russian economic (or political) policies were dominated by foreign financial interests. Moreover, there were several circumstances unrelated to the level of economic development attained elsewhere which made the 1890s a propitious time for investment in Russia. There was, in the first place, the lure of high profits. Government contracts for railway equipment at inflated prices were an obvious attraction. The high level of tariff protection provided considerable opportunities for import substitution. In addition, tariffs themselves encouraged direct foreign investment by firms seeking to operate inside the tariff barriers. Favourable publicity abroad also stimulated the

71

Table 19

GROWTH OF CAPITAL IN RUSSIAN INDUSTRIAL JOINT-STOCK COMPANIES, 1890–1915*

(million roubles)

	1890			1900			1915		
	Total	Foreign	%	Total	Foreign	%	Total	Foreign	%
Mining and metallurgy	85·8	55·7	65	472·2	343·8	72	1,700·0	740·8	63
Engineering and machinery	27·8	13·9	50	177·3	125·6	71		322·7	
Cement, ceramics, glass	6·7	0·2	3	59·1	26·6	45	129·9	18·7	14
Lumber	3·3	0·2	6	17·8	7·8	44	74·4	24·3	32
Chemicals	15·6	6·4	41	93·8	29·3	31	173·2	70·8	41
Food processing	87·6	7·5	8	158·3	11·4	7	447·8	34·6	8
Leather processing	7·3	3·1	43	16·5	5·9	35	54·2	14·5	26
Paper	11·4	1·1	9	31·8	6·1	20	93·2	19·9	20
Textiles	197·6	26·0	13	373·7	71·4	20	729·2	155·0	21
Total	443·1	114·1	26	1,400·5	627·9	45	3,401·9	1,401·3	41

SOURCE: [41] 22–3.

* Figures exclude investment in banking, insurance and commercial companies.

flow of capital; particularly important in this respect was the impact of the political alliance with France in 1894. Similarly, the Entente with Britain in 1907 greatly improved the climate of opinion in Britain about economic prospects in Russia, and a marked increase in the flow of British funds followed.

The success of Russia's repeated excursions to foreign capital markets was greatly facilitated by the Tsarist Government's financial policies. The adoption of the gold standard was seen by Witte and his immediate predecessors as essential to ensure the inflow of foreign capital, and to secure Russia's financial standing among the great powers. It must be remembered that by the 1890s most of the major industrial nations of the world were either already on the gold standard or about to adopt it. Russia's accumulation of gold in the State Bank and State Treasury, achieved through a favourable balance of trade and imports of specie, enabled the stabilisation of the paper rouble and ultimate convertibility. A further factor encouraging the inflow of foreign capital in the 1890s was, as mentioned earlier, the exceptionally low level of world interest rates, which made prospects in Russia seem all the more attractive.

The important role played by the state in shaping Russia's industrialisation has been stressed. But government policies also had adverse effects which must not be overlooked. Fundamental, of course, was the neglect of agriculture. As long as budgetary policies pressed hard on rural incomes, the possibilities of Russian peasants adopting new techniques and raising their productivity were strictly limited. Restricted, too, was the development of domestic demand for industrial products. Criticisms of this nature were frequently made by Russian economists at the time, and by numerous writers, Russian and Western, since. But given the state's objective of fostering rapid industrialisation, were government policies sound?

Kahan [45] has recently suggested that certain government policies may well have had a negative impact on the rate of industrial progress they were supposed to encourage. Taxation policies, for example, were dominated more by short-term fiscal considerations than by the needs of long-term industrial growth. Von Laue, he argues, seriously overestimates the proportion of government revenue channelled into economic develop-

73

ment. The major recipient of such funds as were directed to economic development was railway construction, but even here many state-financed railways had their origin in strategic requirements rather than in the needs of industrial development. Again, government domestic loans competed with loans raised by private industry, and government policies may therefore have contributed to the shortage of domestic capital so often found by Russian industrialists. Tariff policies, too, had obvious adverse effects. The revenue-raising element in the tariffs led to high duties on foodstuffs (tea and salt for example), thereby further reducing the purchasing power of the mass of the population. Duties on raw materials (such as cotton, wool and coal) and on certain capital goods (industrial machinery) raised manufacturing costs considerably. The decision to adopt the gold standard also brought losses, in that the accumulation of gold reserves reduced the availability of investment funds.

As Kahan emphasises, these government policies unquestionably had a stimulating as well as a retarding effect on industrialisation. But to assess the net impact of state activities requires consideration of the losses as well as the gains.

9 Stagnation and Boom, 1900–1913

THE close of the 1890s brought a sharp decline in Russia's industrial growth, and not until well after the revolution of 1905 did boom conditions return once more. The years between 1900 and 1903 were years of crisis in many branches of industry, and hesitant recovery was cut short by the effects of the Russo-Japanese War (1904–5) and the revolution. Only in 1909 was there definite industrial prosperity once more, and between 1909 and 1913 Russia entered another phase of industrial growth comparable with that of the 1890s.

Russian industrialisation after the mid-1880s can thus be seen as following a definite pattern. Ignoring cyclical variations, a long period of growth was succeeded in 1900 by a period of stagnation, followed from about 1907 by recovery once more. Marxist historians stress the importance of the period 1900–13, for it marks for them the phase where capitalism, influenced by the crisis, reached the final state of 'monopoly capitalism' or 'imperialism'. Among Western historians, Gerschenkron also emphasises the importance of discontinuity in Russian industrial-isation. His main concern is to demonstrate the essentially different character of the 1907–13 boom compared with that of the 1890s. From his study of the two periods he draws the conclusion that the Russian economy was progressing on a more 'Western' path, with consumer goods playing a greater role in industrialisation (Table 20 gives some indication of this process).

The industrial crisis which hit Russia at the end of the 1890s showed itself in numerous bankruptcies, sharply falling industrial prices, contracting output (especially in heavy industry), and over-capacity in many industrial sectors. The immediate cause of the recession appears to have been a tightening of the money market from the middle of 1899. This brought the failure of two giant Russian companies, and from this time industrial depression spread quickly. Monetary stringency was world wide,

75

and was the product of several circumstances, including the outbreak of the Boer War and disturbances in the Far East. Rising world interest rates and a slackening in the flow of international investment inevitably had severe repercussions on Russia.

TABLE 20

GROWTH INDICES OF SELECTED INDUSTRIES,
1890–1900 AND 1905–13

	1890	*1900*	*1905*	*1913*
Pig-iron	100	314	100	169
Coal	100	269	100	193
Steel	100	586	100	213
Petroleum	100	275	100	122
Sugar consumption	100	197	100	144
Cotton consumption	100	193	100	155
Low-grade tobacco	100	119	100	147

SOURCE: [13] 452–3.

More fundamental was Russia's agrarian problem. Agricultural productivity remained low and poverty widespread. There is evidence, indeed, that, far from benefiting from the surge of industrialisation in the 1890s, the living standards of the peasants actually fell during this period. Thus a main source of government revenue – itself a mainspring of industrialisation – was based on a precarious foundation. The condition of the Russian peasantry and the influence of agriculture on Russia's industrial development is a complex problem and can only be touched on briefly. It is possible to exaggerate, however, the extent to which government taxation policy squeezed peasant incomes and so destroyed the foundation of government-induced industrialisation. After all, as we have seen, the output of many articles of mass consumption rose substantially in the 1890s. And although indirect taxes were levied on many products, the burden fell most heavily on the urban population rather than on the more self-sufficient agricultural community. Certainly, falling grain prices brought acute distress to many producers, but over much of Russia, in the north and east especially, the peasants were net consumers of grain, and must have gained from falling prices. Above all, agricultural prosperity, and hence to a large extent the prosperity of internal trade, depended on the state of the harvest. Between 1897 and 1901 there was a run of well below-average harvests which hit some of the chief grain-producing areas of the country. Arrears of redemption payments and other taxes rose, and export earnings declined. A rapid rise in emigration to Siberia is evidence not only of the impact of the Trans-Siberian railway, but also of agrarian distress in many parts of Russia at this time. It is noteworthy, however, that cotton-textile production, which catered in the main for the peasant market, was little affected by the crisis. When harvests improved, as they did in 1901 and 1902, purchases of textiles increased also.

The depression, then, affected mainly those branches of heavy industry which had expanded most rapidly in the 1890s. Since government demand and support had been instrumental in the development of these industries, it is to a slackening of state orders that we must look for an explanation of the intensity of the crisis. There was indeed a decline in railway construction after the very rapid upsurge of the late 1890s, and the boom had brought with it a wave of speculation and intense stock-market activity. But by 1900 the Trans-Siberian project was nearing completion, while the decline in tax revenue due to harvest failures was causing the Government to reduce expend-iture in a number of fields of activity. In 1899 state-financed projects had accounted for perhaps 40 per cent of Russian iron consumption. In 1900 came a 10 per cent reduction in government railway orders. Just as rapid railway construction had stimulated so many sectors of the economy in the 1890s, so a slackening of construction had adverse repercussions through-out the economy.

The crisis in Russian industry stimulated the growth of various monopolistic devices for regulating production and sales. Such organisations, unlike German cartels, were rather loose associations concerned almost solely with marketing. In the

1890s there had been a number of attempts at organisation among producers in certain industries, but from 1902 the movement spread rapidly. In 1902 several major groupings were formed, including Prodamet in the metallurgical industry. In the following years similar syndicates were established in a wide variety of different industries. Produgol (1906) controlled sales of Donetz coal, Prodvagon (1904) that of railway carriages, Med (1907) that of copper, Krovlya (1907) that of numerous products of the Ural metallurgical industries. By 1914 there were over 150 such associations, and they covered not only the mining and metallurgical sectors but also certain branches of light industry such as cotton textiles.

A feature of the Russian syndicates was their extensive control of operations within individual industries. Thus Med controlled the marketing of virtually all of Russia's copper industry, while Prodamet in 1913 marketed the products of the thirty major metallurgical plants which accounted for some 90 per cent of total output. Such instances could be multiplied, although not all syndicates were as dominant as these. The growth of such associations was facilitated by the already highly concentrated structure of Russian industry, and the development of syndicates fostered further concentration. The existence of large-scale foreign and banking interests in many branches of Russian industry appears also to have encouraged the formation of marketing associations as a remedy against the losses entailed by overproduction in the crisis of 1900–3.

It is difficult to assess the impact of syndicates on Russian industrial growth. Soviet historians place considerable emphasis on their development, since they are seen as a crucial phase in the transition to 'monopoly capitalism'. On the other hand, no study exists which attempts to quantify their impact on prices or production. The trend of industrial prices was certainly upwards between the 1905 revolution and the outbreak of the First World War, but this was a general tendency observable in both syndicated and non-syndicated industries alike. Moreover, competition did not disappear. Powerful concerns remained outside the syndicates in most industrial sectors. Yet it is indisputable that the formation of syndicates often had at least a short-term influence on the price level, and during the 1909–13 boom complaints that the syndicates were deliberately restricting output in order to raise prices were too numerous to be ignored.

By the outbreak of the First World War, Russia's industries had grown considerably from their 1900 level, and most sectors participated in this development. The official statistics of factory industry show that the industrial labour force expanded by about one million in these years, to approximately 3 million in 1914. According to the industrial census of 1908, the total value of the output of 'factory' industry was nearly 5,000 million roubles, and in 1913 it stood at roughly 6,000 million roubles compared with under 3,000 million in 1897. And the value of small-scale industry was probably still roughly one-third that of large industry.

The overall growth rate of industry between 1906 and 1913 was rather more than 6 per cent per annum. Heavy industries continued to grow rapidly. Coal output grew from 986 to 2,200 million poods between 1900 and 1913, pig-iron from 179 to 283 million poods, and manufactured iron and steel from 134 to 247 million poods. (Oil production, however, failed to reach again its 1901 peak of 706 million poods, being only 561 million poods in 1913.) Consumer-goods industries likewise showed considerable expansion. Cotton consumption increased from 16·0 to 25·9 million poods, while the work-force in cotton textiles rose from 391,000 in 1901 to 556,000 by 1914. Foreign trade also showed a marked growth, with exports rising from 716 million roubles in 1900 to 1,520 million in 1913, and imports rising over the same period from 626 to 1,374 million roubles.

As Gerschenkron has shown, the increased pace of activity in the years 1907–13 marked a boom of a rather different character from that of the 1890s. Gerschenkron emphasises the diminished role of the Government and the correspondingly greater role of consumer demand in fostering industrial activity. The general conditions of the peasants improved, enabling them to provide a greater market for domestic manufactured products. At the same time, fundamental changes in agricultural organisation reduced the importance of the *mir*, and therefore stimulated the growth of the industrial labour force. In the finance of industry the banking system came to play an increasingly important part.

The diminished role of the Government can be seen in the

79

slackening growth of railway construction. Between 1907 and 1913 an average of only 933 km. of track was laid annually. During the 1890s Russia's metallurgical industries had depended to an overwhelming extent on government contracts for railway development. After 1907 a larger part of demand for the output of Russia's capital-goods industries came instead from the requirements of consumer-goods industries. Per capita consumption of many basic articles grew in these years, thus showing the buoyancy of the non-governmental sector. The relative weight of 'heavy' industries in the economy, which had grown so rapidly in the 1890s, ceased to grow thereafter if value of product is taken as an indicator.

Several factors underlay the growth of domestic demand. As Gerschenkron emphasises, the results of the 1890s boom, involving massive investment in an industrial infrastructure, permanently raised the productive capacity of the Russian economy. The industrial base and general level of technology in Russia were substantially higher in 1906 than they had been in 1890. At the same time conditions among the rural population improved in these years. Fundamental to the improvement were better terms of trade for agricultural producers. Grain prices, and those of other farm products, rose relative to prices of industrial goods both on domestic and world markets. Overall, the general price level in Russia increased by some 29 per cent between 1900 and 1913, while the prices of agricultural products rose by 41 per cent.

Among the results of the social unrest in the early years of the new century was legislation to improve the lot of the peasantry. In 1905 redemption payments were abolished, and in 1906 and 1910 came the famous Stolypin land reforms. These reforms permitted the voluntary disbanding of the *mir* and the abolition of joint land holding and joint responsibility for tax payments. Stolypin's reforms were aimed at creating a prosperous class of peasants which, it was hoped, would provide a firm basis of political support for the Tsarist Government. To this end, the state also took other steps to improve peasant agriculture. The Peasant Land Bank, founded in 1885, was encouraged to buy gentry land and resell it to peasants. Between 1906 and 1915 over 4 million dessyatins of land were purchased by peasants in this way, compared with under one million in the previous decade. The Government also encouraged the migration of peasants to Siberia after 1905, and by 1913 Western Siberia had become an important dairying region based on a remarkable development of peasant marketing co-operatives. As Tokmakoff has pointed out, however, the outbreak of the First World War renders any final evaluation of the success of Stolypin's land reforms impossible.

Undoubtedly, the Russian banks came to play an increasing role in industrial investment in the years after 1907, yet the difference in the sources of investment in the 1890s and the 1907–13 boom is not so clear-cut as is sometimes supposed. Dr Crisp [36] has shown that joint-stock banks were active in industrial development in the 1890s, and that they provided an important channel for the flow of foreign capital into certain sectors of the economy. There existed a close connection between the banking structure and the Russian Treasury, so that the distinction between state finance on the one hand and 'private' bank finance on the other cannot be too finely drawn. The Government as a direct source of investment was by no means dormant in the second boom period. State railway construction continued, although on a reduced level. And there was an increasing emphasis on government investment in the agricultural sector. There were, for example, numerous dock and harbour improvements at the main grain ports, and the Government also undertook the construction of grain elevators in various parts of the country.

Elements of continuity between the boom periods also need to be emphasised. Foreign capital continued to play a major role, although proportionally domestic capital became more significant. As in the 1890s, heavy industries continued to expand rapidly, and at the peak of the boom between 1909 and 1913 they once more outpaced consumer-goods industries. The geographical concentration of production of heavy industries in the Ukraine also continued. By 1913 the southern provinces produced 72 per cent of Russia's iron ore, 70 per cent of her coal and 57 per cent of her iron and steel. In the oil industry, however, output never regained its 1901 level, and the Baku districts, which had been severely damaged in the numerous disturbances between 1901 and 1905, lost ground to new producing regions.

Concentration of production in large-scale units became an even more marked feature of Russian industrialisation, and was stimulated by the new cartel arrangements. Of an estimated 2,243,800 workers in enterprises employing more than twenty workers throughout Russian industry in 1913, no fewer than 40 per cent were concentrated in plants employing more than 1,000. In 1901 the figure had been 32·1 per cent. And over this period the average number of workers in each enterprise expanded from 148 to 191. The process of concentration is shown in Table 21, which is based on official data covering most of large-scale industry.

1913, the last year of peace, saw boom conditions in Russia, a boom based on more secure foundations than those of the 1890s. In three decades Russia had industrialised on a more rapid scale than any other country during that period. Her industrialisation, from being 'forced' in the 1890s in a manner reminiscent of Peter the Great, was becoming more spontaneous by the outbreak of the war. Without the war, would such a development have continued? Certainly, there were many disquieting features of the Russian economy. The agrarian problem remained, and the success of Stolypin's 'wager on the strong' must remain imponderable. Also, the growing proletariat, ever more concentrated in the expanding urban centres, and often living and working in deplorable conditions, was a major potential threat to Russia's political and economic system. Gerschenkron suggests that Russian industrialisation might well have continued along the lines of the 'Western' path that he has noted as a feature of the 1907–13 boom period. But von Laue has challenged this view, and argues that the main forces behind the rapid post-1907 growth rate were in decline by the outbreak of war.[15]

Had the Russian economy 'taken off' by 1913? Again, no straightforward answer is possible. Even if one accepts the usefulness of Rostow's concept, the inadequacy of the data makes it impossible to judge. Certainly, by 1913 the level of Russia's per capita income marked her as the poorest of the world's great

[15] See the discussion in von Laue [78].

TABLE 21

CONCENTRATION IN RUSSIAN INDUSTRY, 1901–14

Size of plant	1901				1914			
	Enterprises	%	Workers	%	Enterprises	%	Workers	%
Under 100 workers	15,168	83·9	414,785	24·4	11,117	78·4	348,876	17·8
101–500 workers	2,288	12·6	492,095	28·9	2,253	16·1	504,440	25·7
501–1,000 workers	403	2·2	269,133	15·8	432	3·1	296,347	15·1
Over 1,000 workers	243	1·3	525,637	30·9	344	2·4	811,197	41·4
Total	18,102	100	1,701,650	100	14,146	100	1,960,860	100

SOURCE: [16] 217,

powers and one of the poorest countries in Europe. It is in industrial growth that Russia achieved most, although even here, as we saw in the Introduction, the structure of Russia's industries was hardly 'modern' by comparison with other advanced nations. Yet in a few decades much had been accomplished. No explanation of Russia's industrial growth under the Soviet regime after 1917 would be complete without taking into account the industrial base inherited from Tsarist days.

Bibliography

GENERAL NOTE

THIS bibliography does not pretend to be comprehensive. Its main purpose is to list some of the more important books and articles published in English on the subject, and, on a far more restricted scale, to note some of the principal general studies in Russian. A few titles in French have also been included.

There exists no satisfactory recent textbook on Russian economic history covering the period under review. The basic work is that by the Marxist economic historian, P. I. LYASHCHENKO, *Istoriia Narodnogo Khozyaistva SSSR*, 2 vols (Moscow, 3rd ed., 1952) [1]. The 1939 edition of this work is available in English translation, *A History of the National Economy of Russia to the 1917 Revolution* (New York, 1949) [2]. Also useful is B. GILLE, *Histoire Économique et Sociale de la Russie du Moyen Age au XXe Siècle* (Paris, 1949) [3]. J. MAVOR, *An Economic History of Russia*, 2 vols (London, 2nd ed., 1925) [4] is very dated in approach and content, although still valuable on institutional problems. A recent study by W. L. BLACKWELL, *The Beginnings of Russian Industrialisation, 1800–1860* (Princeton, 1968) [5] is a scholarly work containing a mass of information and a vast bibliography. A. BAYKOV, 'The Economic Development of Russia', *Economic History Review*, VII (Dec 1954) 137–49 [6] is an important interpretative article. R. PORTAL, 'The Industrialisation of Russia' in *The Cambridge Economic History*, vol. VI, part 2 (Cambridge, 1966) pp. 801–72 [7] is a useful survey of industrial growth, while an important quantitative study is provided by R. W. GOLDSMITH, 'The Economic Growth of Tsarist Russia, 1860–1913', *Economic Development and Cultural Change*, IX (1961) 441–75 [8]. V. K. YATSUNSKY, 'Main Features of Industrialisation in Russia before 1917', in *First International Conference of Economic History* (Paris, 1960) pp. 297–307 [9] is an outline survey by a well-known Marxist economic historian.

Students should also read the economic chapters in some of the major general history textbooks, such as M. T. FLORINSKY, *Russia: A History and an Interpretation*, 2 vols (New York, 1953) [10], and his *Russia: A Short History* (New York, 1964) [11]; also N. V. RIASONOVSKY, *A History of Russia* (Oxford, 2nd ed., 1969) [12].

Among Russian-language textbooks P. A. KHROMOV, *Ekonomicheskoe Razvitie Rossii v XIX–XX Vekakh* (Moscow, 1950) [13] is particu-

85

larly useful, containing numerous statistical tables drawn largely from official data. See also the collections of articles in *Istoriya SSSR*, 2 vols (Moscow, 1956–9) [14] and F. POLYANSKII *et. al* (eds), *Istoriya Narodnogo Khozyaistva SSSR* (Moscow, 1960) [15]. Further important studies are A. F. YAKOVLEV, *Ekonomischeskie Krizisy v Rossii* (Moscow, 1955) [16] (a primarily statistical analysis of the trade cycle in Russia during the nineteenth and early twentieth centuries); P. G. LIUBIMIROV, *Ocherki po Istorii Promyshlennosti* (Moscow, 1947) [17]; and the collections of some of S. G. STRUMILIN's most important articles in *Ocherki Ekonomicheskoi Istorii Rossii* (Moscow, 1960) [18] and *Ocherki Ekonomicheskoe Istorii Rossii i SSSR* (Moscow, 1966) [19]. Much useful information will also be found in V. I. LENIN, *The Development of Capitalism in Russia* (English translation, Moscow, 1956) [20] and M. I. TUGAN-BARANOVSKII, *Russkaia Fabrika v Proshlom i Nastoiashchem*, vol. I (St Petersburg, 1898) [21] (the 1907 edition is available in English translation, entitled *The Russian Factory in the Nineteenth Century*).

Studies of particular industries include R. PORTAL, *L'Oural au XVIIIe Siècle* (Paris, 1950) [22]; S. G. STRUMILIN, *Istoriia Chernoi Metallurgii v SSSR*, vol. I (Moscow, 1954) [23]; and K. A. PAZHITNOV, *Ocherki Istorii Tekstil'noi Promyshlennosti Dorevoliutsionnoi Rossii* (Moscow, 1958) [24]. A great deal of factual information on the development of Russian industries and other aspects of the economy will be found in J. CRAWFORD (ed.), *The Industries of Russia*, 5 vols (St Petersburg, 1893) [25]; A. RAFFALOVICH (ed.), *Russia: Its Trade and Commerce* (London, 1918) [26]; M. W. KOVALEVSKY (ed.), *La Russie à la Fin du 19e Siècle* (Paris, 1900) [27]; and L. TEGOBORSKII, *Commentaries on the Productive Forces of Russia*, 2 vols (London, 1855–6) [28].

Fundamental to a study of Russian economic history are the numerous interpretative articles by A. GERSCHENKRON. *Economic Backwardness in Historical Perspective* (Cambridge, Mass., 1962) [29] contains some of his major studies. See also 'The Rate of Industrial Growth in Russia since 1885', *Journal of Economic History*, supp. 7 (1947) pp. 144–74 [30]; 'Agrarian Policies and Industrialisation in Russia, 1861–1917', in *The Cambridge Economic History*, vol. VI, part 2 (Cambridge, 1966) pp. 706–800 [31]; and *Europe in the Russian Mirror: Four Lectures in Economic History* (Cambridge, 1970) [32].

The following select list will be found helpful on particular topics.

SELECT LIST

[33] E. AMES, 'A Century of Russian Railroad Construction,

86

1837–1936', *American Slavic and East European Review*, VI (1945) 57–74.

[34] J. BLUM, *Lord and Peasant in Russia from the Ninth to the Nineteenth Century* (Princeton, 1961).

[35] O. CRISP, 'Russian Financial Policy and the Gold Standard at the End of the Nineteenth Century', *Economic History Review*, VI (1953) 156–72.

[36] O. CRISP, 'Russia, 1860–1914', in R. B. CAMERON (ed.), *Banking in the Early Stages of Industrialisation* (Oxford, 1967) pp. 183–238.

[37] O. CRISP, 'Some Problems of French Investment in Russian Joint Stock Companies, 1894–1914', *Slavonic and East European Review*, XXXV (Dec 1956) 223–40.

[38] O. CRISP, 'French Investment in Russian Joint Stock Companies, 1894–1914', *Business History*, II (June 1960) 75–90.

[39] O. CRISP, 'The State Peasants under Nicholas I', *Slavonic Review*, XVII (1959) 387–412.

[40] H. J. ELLISON, 'Economic Modernisation in Imperial Russia: Purposes and Achievements', *Journal of Economic History*, XXV (Dec 1965) 523–40.

[41] L. EVENTOV, *Innostrannye Kapitaly v Russkoi Promyshlennosti* (Moscow, 1931).

[42] A. GERSCHENKRON, 'The Beginnings of Russian Industrialisation?', *Soviet Studies* (Apr 1970) pp. 507–15.

[43] M. GORDON, *Workers Before and After Lenin* (New York, 1941).

[44] A. KAHAN, 'Entrepreneurship in the Early Development of Iron Manufacturing in Russia', *Economic Development and Cultural Change*, X (July 1962) 395–422.

[45] A. KAHAN, 'Government Policies and the Industrialisation of Russia', *Journal of Economic History*, XXVII (Dec 1967) 460–77.

[46] A. KAHAN, 'Continuity in Economic Activity and Policy during the Post-Petrine Period in Russia', *Journal of Economic History*, XXV (Mar 1965) 61–85.

[47] V. KLIUCHEVSKY, *Course of Russian History*, translated from Russian (New York, 1911–31).

[48] K. KONONENKO, *Ukraine and Russia: A History of the Economic Relations between Ukraine and Russia, 1654–1917* (Milwaukee, 1958).

[49] KON'YUNKTURNI INSTITUT, *Mirovoe Khozyaistvo, Statisticheskii Sbornik za 1913–25 gg.* (Moscow, 1926).

[50] I. M. KULISHER, 'La Grande Industrie aux XVIIe et XVIIIe Siècles: France, Allemagne, Russie', *Annales d'Histoire Économique et Sociale*, III (Jan 1931) 11–46.

[51] J. P. McKay, *Pioneers for Profit: Foreign Entrepreneurship and Russian Industrialisation, 1885–1913* (Chicago, 1970).

[52] M. S. Miller, *The Economic Development of Russia, 1905–1914* (London, 1926).

[53] P. Ol', *Innostrannye Kapitali v Rossii* (Moscow, 1922).

[54] L. A. Owen, *The Russian Peasant Movement, 1906–1917* (London, 1937).

[55] W. W. Pintner, *Economic Policy under Nicholas I* (New York, 1967).

[56] M. N. Pokrovsky, *Brief History of Russia,* 2 vols (London, 1933).

[57] R. Portal, 'The Problem of an Industrial Revolution in Russia in the Nineteenth Century', in S. Harcave (ed.), *Readings in Russian History* (New York, 1962) ii 22–9.

[58] A. G. Rashin, *Naselenie Rossii za 100 let (1811–1913 gg.):* *Statisticheskie Ocherki* (Moscow, 1956).

[59] A. G. Rashin, *Formirovanie Promyshlennogo Proletariata v Rossii* (Moscow, 1940).

[60] N. V. Riasonovsky, *A History of Russia* (Oxford, 2nd ed., 1969).

[61] G. V. Rimlinger, 'The Expansion of the Labour Market in Capitalist Russia, 1861–1917', *Journal of Economic History,* xxi (June 1961) 208–15.

[62] G. V. Rimlinger, 'Autocracy and Factory Order in Early Russian Industrialisation', *Journal of Economic History,* xx (Mar 1960) 67–92.

[63] G. T. Robinson, *Rural Russia under the Old Regime* (New York, 1932).

[64] H. Rosovsky, 'The Serf Entrepreneur in Russia', *Explorations in Entrepreneurial History,* vi (1953–4) 207–29.

[65] M. K. Rozhkova (ed.), *Ocherki Ekonomicheskoi Istorii Rossii Pervoi Poloviny XIX Veka* (Moscow, 1959).

[66] A. A. Skerpan, 'The Russian National Economy and Emancipation', in A. D. Ferguson and A. Levin (eds), *Essays in Russian History* (Hamden, Conn., 1964).

[67] J. D. Sontag, 'Tsarist Debts and Tsarist Foreign Policy', *Slavic Review,* xxvii 4 (Dec 1968) 531–3.

[68] S. G. Strumilin, 'Industrial Crises in Russia, 1847–67', in F. Crouzet *et al.* (eds), *Essays in European Economic History, 1789–1914* (London, 1969) pp. 155–78.

[69] G. Tokmakoff, 'Stolypin's Agrarian Reform: An Appraisal', *Russian Review* (Apr 1971) pp. 124–38.

[70] D. W. TREADGOLD, *The Great Siberian Migration* (Princeton, 1957).

[71] L. VOLIN, *A Century of Russian Agriculture: From Alexander II to Khrushchev* (Cambridge, Mass., 1970).

[72] T. H. VON LAUE, 'Russian Peasants in the Factory, 1892–1904', *Journal of Economic History*, XXI (March 1961) 61–80.

[73] T. H. VON LAUE, 'The High Cost and the Gamble of the Witte System: A Chapter in the Industrialisation of Russia', *Journal of Economic History*, XIII 4 (1953) 425–48.

[74] T. H. VON LAUE, 'A Secret Memorandum of Sergei Witte on the Industrialisation of Imperial Russia', *Journal of Modern History*, XXVI (March 1954).

[75] T. H. VON LAUE, 'The State and the Economy', in C. E. BLACK (ed.), *The Transformation of Russian Society* (Cambridge, Mass., 1960) pp. 209–25.

[76] T. H. VON LAUE, *Sergei Witte and the Industrialisation of Russia* (New York, 1963).

[77] T. H. VON LAUE, 'Russian Labour between Field and Factory, 1892–1903', *California Slavic Studies*, III (1964).

[78] T. H. VON LAUE, 'Problems of Industrialisation', in T. STAVROU (ed.), *Russia under the Last Tsar* (Minneapolis, 1969) pp. 117–53.

[79] J. N. WESTWOOD, *A History of Russian Railways* (London, 1964).

[80] J. N. WESTWOOD, 'John Hughes and Russian Metallurgy', *Economic History Review*, XVII (Apr 1965) 564–9.

[81] B. YAKOVLEV, 'Vozniknovenie i Etapy Razvitiya Kapitalisticheskogo Uklada v Rossii', *Voprosy Istorii*, no. 9 (1950) 91–104.

[82] G. L. YANEY, 'The Concept of the Stolypin Land Reforms', *Slavic Review*, XXIII (June 1964) 275–93.

[83] V. K. YATSUNSKY, 'Promyshlenii Perevorot v Rossii', *Voprosy Istorii*, no. 12 (1952) 48–70.

[84] V. K. YATSUNSKY, 'Formation en Russie de la Grande Industrie Textile sur la Base de la Production Rurale', in *Second International Conference of Economic History* (Paris, 1962) pp. 365–76.

[85] S. O. ZAGORSKY, *State Control of Industry in Russia during the War* (New York, 1928).

[86] R. E. ZELNIK, 'The Peasant and the Factory', in W. VUCINICH (ed.), *The Peasant in Nineteenth Century Russia* (Stanford, 1968) pp. 158–90.

H. Barkai, 'The Macro-Economics of Tsarist Russia in the Industrialization Era', *Journal of Economic History*, xxxiii (June 1973).

J. H. Bater, *St Petersburg: Industrialization and Change* (London, 1976).

O. Crisp, *Studies in the Russian Economy Before 1914* (London, 1976).

J. T. Fuhrmann, *The Origins of Capitalism in Russia: Industry and Progress in the Sixteenth and Seventeenth Centuries* (Chicago, 1972).

G. Garvy, 'Banking Under the Tsars and the Soviets', *Journal of Economic History*, xxxii (1972).

R. Girault, *Emprunts Russes et Investissements Français en Russie, 1887–1914* (Paris, 1973).

P. R. Gregory, 'Economic Growth and Structural Change in Tsarist Russia: A Case of Modern Economic Growth?', *Soviet Studies*, xxiii 3 (1972).

P. R. Gregory, 'Russian National Income in 1913 – Some Insights into Russian Economic Development', *Quarterly Journal of Economics*, iii (August 1976).

P. R. Gregory, 'Some Empirical Comments on the Relative Backwardness Hypothesis: The Russian Case', *Economic Development and Cultural Change*, xxii 4 (July 1974).

J. Metzer, 'Railroad Development and Market Integration: The Case of Tsarist Russia', *Journal of Economic History*, xxxiv 3 (September 1974).

C. M. White, 'The Concept of Social Saving in Theory and Practice', *Economic History Review*, xxix 1 (February 1976).

R. E. Zelnik, *Labor and Society in Tsarist Russia: The Factory Workers of St Petersburg* (Stanford, 1971).

Index

agricultural productivity, 47 ff.,
73, 76
agriculture, 11, 18, 28, 32, 36,
46, 49, 54, 56, 63, 73, 76–7,
80–1
Alexander II, 45

balance of trade, 56–7, 63–4,
73
banking, 41, 67, 71, 78–9, 81
barshchina, *see* serf obligations
budget, 17, 37, 61 ff., 73, 76
Bunge, N. K., 64

canals, 32
Catherine II, 26, 29
Caucasus, 20, 45, 55, 59–60,
66, 70; *see also* oil industry
climate, 18, 44, 55
coal industry, 13, 18, 20, 41,
45, 51, 55, 76, 78–9, 81
cotton, raw, 35, 37, 52–3, 56,
66
'cotton famine', 53
cotton textiles, 12–13, 15, 29,
33, 35, 37 ff., 52–3, 56, 66,
68–9, 71, 76 ff.
Crimean War (1854–6), 42, 62

Donetz, *see* Ukraine

Emancipation of the Serfs,
14–15, 20, 31, 44 ff., 50, 52–3
entrepreneurs, 23–4, 26, 38,
44, 58

famine of 1891, 54
foreign investment, 19, 57 ff.,
67, 69 ff., 76, 81
foreign trade, 11, 20, 27, 32,
36 ff., 55–6, 63, 79

Gerschenkron, A., 14, 22, 42,
45, 61, 68, 75, 79, 82
gold standard, 62, 73–4
government economic policy,
21 ff., 28, 55 ff., 61 ff., 68,
73–4, 76 ff., 80–1; *see also*
Peter the Great; Witte, S.
government statistics, 15–16

handicraft industries, 12, 15,
18, 21, 27, 30, 32, 40, 42,
45, 64–5, 69
Hughes, J., 58

industrial census, 15, 64–5, 79
industrial concentration, 38, 42,
58, 67–8, 78, 81–3
industrial growth rate, 45–6,
50, 53–4, 64, 66, 75–6, 79, 82
'industrial revolution', 20, 31,
41
industrial syndicates, 77–8, 82
iron and steel, *see* metallurgy
iron industry, 27, 29–30, 41, 45,
51–2, 55, 57–9, 62, 67, 76,
77, 79, 81
Ivanovo, 29, 38

joint-stock companies, 33, 38,
53, 70–2

STUDIES IN ECONOMIC HISTORY

Some Opinions on Published Titles

INFLATION IN TUDOR AND EARLY STUART ENGLAND
R. B. Outhwaite

Dr Outhwaite has provided a valuable commentary on the debate, for which students and teachers of the subject will be grateful. *Economica.*

... both the specialist economic historian and the non-specialist should find much to interest them in this admirable little book. *British Book News.*

THE ECONOMIC EFFECTS OF THE TWO WORLD WARS ON BRITAIN
Alan S. Milward

Students will find it a convenient introduction to some of the more interesting issues which have been the subject of debate, and for those who are looking for a research topic there are some helpful signposts. *Economic Journal.*

Professor Milward has had a harder job than most of his predecessors in this excellent new series . . . [his] device has been to weave . . . tendentially disparate strands of enquiry into a single main line of argument – that of the effects of the wars upon income distribution. It has enabled him to give his exposition clarity without sacrificing scholarly caution. *Times Educational Supplement.*

THE DECLINE OF SERFDOM IN MEDIEVAL ENGLAND
R. H. Hilton

... this essay is useful for its excellent regional survey of peasant tenure and for the synthesis of much detail from theses and monographs. *English Historical Review.*

BRITISH POPULATION GROWTH 1700–1850
M. W. Flinn

Professor Flinn's lucid and brief introduction admirably does what the 'Studies in Economic History' series sets out to achieve: to 'indicate the full scope of the particular problem as it has been opened by research and distinguish what conclusions can be drawn in the present state of knowledge'. *Times Literary Supplement.*
This survey of the state of the debate is a model of its kind. It discusses the quality of the statistics, the main issues in question and the implications of the more recent work with a clarity and precision which will illuminate even those who have been following the debate. For students it will be an invaluable introduction and guide to a complex literature. *British Book News.*

THE OLD POOR LAW 1795–1834
J. D. Marshall

Indexed, footnoted and up-to-date, this 50-page pamphlet clearly portrays the workings of the poor law immediately before the great reforms of 1834. A controversial theme, fair-mindedly treated. *New Society.*

SOME MACMILLAN BOOKS ON RUSSIA AND THE SOVIET UNION

HISTORY OF IMPERIAL AND SOVIET RUSSIA
Paul Dukes (in preparation)

THE RISE OF THE ROMANOVS
Vasili Klyuchevsky

PETER THE GREAT
Vasili Klyuchevsky

THE CHURCH REFORM OF PETER THE GREAT
James Cracraft

CATHERINE THE GREAT: A PROFILE
Marc Raeff (ed.)

THE EASTERN QUESTION, 1744–1923
M. S. Anderson

A HISTORY OF RUSSIA, 1812–1945
Graham Stevenson

BREST-LITOVSK: THE FORGOTTEN PEACE
John W. Wheeler-Bennett

1917: BEFORE AND AFTER
E. H. Carr

A HISTORY OF SOVIET RUSSIA
E. H. Carr
   The Bolshevik Revolution, 1917–1923 (3 vols.)
   The Interregnum, 1923–1924 (1 vol.)
   Socialism in One Country, 1924–1926 (4 vols.)
   Foundations of a Planned Economy (2 vols.)

THE GREAT TERROR
Robert Conquest

SOVIET EMPIRE: THE TURKS OF CENTRAL ASIA
AND COMMUNISM
Olaf Caroe

FERMENT IN THE UKRAINE
Michael Browne (ed.)

COMMUNISM AND COLONIALISM
Walter Kolarz

THE EMERGENCE OF THE SUPERPOWERS:
A SHORT COMPARATIVE HISTORY OF THE
U.S.A. AND THE U.S.S.R.
Paul Dukes